POWER PAK
for Preschool Programs

Skills-Based Activity Units
for the Entire Year

by Claudette Gronski and Judith Meeker

Incentive Publications, Inc.
Nashville, Tennessee

Illustrated by Mary Hamilton
Edited by Susan Oglander

Library of Congress Catalog Number 83-83187
ISBN 0-86530-025-9

UNITS OF STUDY

PREFACE

There is a growing need for a quality preschool curriculum in today's society. An increase in women employed outside the home and the growing emphasis on learning basic skills and concepts at a young age, point out the need for a comprehensive, well-structured preschool curriculum. The activities collected in this book have been drawn from teachers actually working in the preschool setting.

The units that follow are geared for children 2½ to 5 years of age. Younger children may enjoy sharing in the different activities; but because of their limited capabilities, they should not be forced to participate. Creative play is essential to their development. It should be encouraged and may be scheduled while the older children are engaged in learning activities.

The activities are categorized with an eye to developing the whole child, not just a specific area of ability. The activities encompass language development, sensory awareness, large and small motor development, spatial and number concepts, art and music appreciation, practical life skills, nature and science, visual and auditory discrimination and social personal growth.

Each unit contains a list of activities and directions which can be used to suit your individual needs.
> 1. You may use them as weekly lesson plans.
> 2. You may select those that you feel are appropriate for your age group and situation to supplement your own activities.
> 3. You may use this as a reference to supplement your established curriculum.

Many of the activities will need to be repeated within the week to reinforce the concept in the young child's mind. It is suggested that the learning aspect should be conducted in the morning, as afternoons are best suited for naps, free play and other motor activities.

These units provide activities sufficient for a full year's curriculum.

FAMILY AND FRIENDS

NOTES

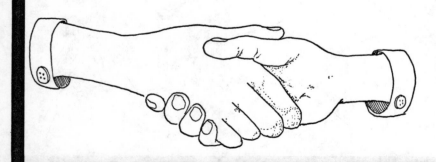

FAMILY AND FRIENDS

———————— Vocabulary ————————

Young, old, big, little, family, friends, home, school, red, yellow, orange, green, blue, purple, brown, black.

Family Pictures

Have the children bring a picture of themselves with their family. Share pictures with peers. Put the pictures on a bulletin board with the name of the child printed underneath. Pictures can remain on the bulletin board all year and provide security for the child in his new environment.

Learning Each Other's Names

Prior to this exercise, you should collect a snapshot of each child from his parents, or take a snapshot of each child yourself. Tack the snapshots to the bulletin board. Seat the children in front of the bulletin board and let them recite the name of each child as the picture of that child is pointed to. Place the name card of the child under the picture to refresh the children's memories. Then, take the name cards from the board and distribute them to the children. Each child takes the name card he has been given and tries to sound out the name, and then puts the name card under the correct picture.

Who Am I?

Play a guessing game with the children. Describe someone in the room by hair color, eye color and clothing. Keep giving verbal clues until the children guess who it is.

FINGER

———————————————— **"Grandma's Glasses"** ————————————————

"Here are grandma's glasses, (circle fingers around eyes to make glasses)

Here is grandma's cap, (Make big circle with fingers & thumbs & hold on head for cap)

This is the way she folds her hands, (fold hands and put in lap)

And lays them in her lap."
(repeat for other family members)

"Here Is a Ball"

"Here is a ball (join index finger and thumb of one hand to form circle)

And here's a ball; (same with other hand)

And a great big ball, you see. (make circle of arms overhead)
Shall we count them?
Are you ready?
One, two, three!" (repeat ball formations as you count)

——————— **Sorting Sizes** ———————————————————————

MATH

Demonstrate the concepts of big and little by trying to put objects of varying sizes into a uniform container. (A coffee can is good.) Make sure you have some very small objects (marble, bean, toothpick) as well as some very large ones (big ball, box, big block). Using a big and little size of the same kind of object is helpful (big and little ball, big and little box). The little objects should fit into the container and the big ones should not. Ask the children to predict if the object will fit into the container. Emphasize vocabulary.

Variation: Invite the children to help you arrange a set of objects from biggest to littlest. Use a variety of different objects, making sure there is an obvious size difference and progression. Nesting blocks or nesting barrels (cans, bottles) would work well. Next, use nesting blocks for predicting big and little. Blindfold a child and place a big block and a little block in his hands. Can he point out the big one? The little one? In this activity, the child is actually feeling size difference. Stress vocabulary.

Young and Old

To understand the concept of young and old, talk about the ages of the children and the teachers. If one child is four years old, count it out on your fingers. Compare it to a three-year-old. Show them that four is more than three. The four-year-old is older; the three-year-old is younger. Continue comparing the ages of all the children. Tell them your age, and count it out with sticks so they can see it; you're the oldest. Use the sticks to compare ages—one stick for each year of age. The set having more sticks is older; the set with fewer sticks is younger. Emphasize vocabulary.

Variation: Find a picture with many people in it. Be sure there is a significant age range. Discuss the people, determining who is young and who is old. Use comparatives such as young, younger, youngest; old, older, oldest. What can a very young person do that a very old person cannot do? (run fast). What can an older person do that a younger person cannot do? (write).

MATH
continued

─────────── **Bubbles** ───────────

Buy a dozen jars of commerical bubble solution and enough wire "dippers" for the whole class. Pass them out to the children. Now, dip the dipper into the bubble jar to collect a film of solution and demonstrate how to blow or wave the stick gently. Look at the "rainbow" of colors on the dipper! Go outside and fill the air with bubbles!

SCIENCE

─────────── **"Where Is _____?"** ───────────
An activity for learning new "friends' " names

"Where is _____?"
"Where is _____?"

"There she/he is!"
"There she/he is!"
(point gently to child)

"Mary Wore Her Red Dress"
"Mary wore her **red dress, red dress, red dress.**
Mary wore her **red dress,** all day long.

Nathan wore his **blue pants, blue pants, blue pants.**
Nathan wore his **blue pants,** all day long."
(for learning colors and for individual recognition)

Finger Painting

The practical value of this activity is in the experience. The "product" is secondary. Children derive a great deal of satisfaction from making their own play tools and materials. Making finger paints feels good to the children and develops skills of measuring and mixing. Make finger paints with the children, allowing them to measure flour, mix and fill containers. These paints are washable and can be stored in the refrigerator for a long time.

Recipe

12 ounce box of cold water starch
12 ounce box of soap flakes
Mix together. Slowly add 2 cups of cold water. Beat to consistency of whipped potatoes. Add powdered tempera paint and store in small jars.

Ways to maximize the experience:
- freedom to work on tabletop without paper. (Plastic sheets can be taped to tabletops to protect them from staining.)
- put paper in tray, thus giving the child freedom within a boundary.
- tape paper to the table to prevent movement of paper.
- use different textures (soap flakes, starch recipes, shaving cream, puddings, salt, sand, sawdust).

Weigh and Measure

Discuss the many different ways of recording changes in growth. Explain and show how a scale and tape measure are used. You may also want to discuss nutrition and dental hygiene with the children. Weighing and measuring should be done twice a year.

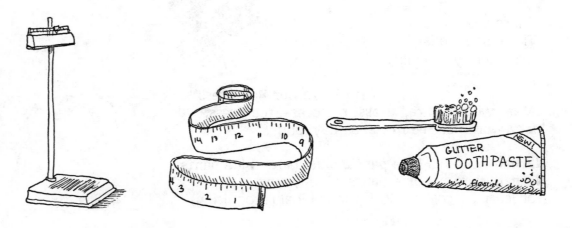

COOK

TO LEARN

—————— **Fruited Gelatin** ——————

Follow the directions given on box of gelatin. Add cut up bananas, apples, or canned fruit cocktail. Pour mixture into small paper cups and place in refrigerator to firm.

Finger Gelatin

4 packets of unflavored gelatin
3 3-ounce packages of flavored gelatin
5 cups water

Dissolve flavored gelatin in 4 cups boiling water. Mix unflavored packets into 1 cup tap water. Add to dissolved mixture. Mix well. Pour into a 9 x 13 x 1 inch pan. Refrigerate until set. Pieces of gelatin can be held in the child's hand to eat.

Gelatin/Pudding Parfait

Follow directions on the boxes of gelatin. Place gelatin in refrigerator to thicken. Follow directions on the back of pudding box. After gelatin thickens, layer pudding and gelatin in small plastic glasses. Talk about textures and the substances changing from a liquid to a solid.

Banana Delight

Slice bananas. Mix with sour cream and a spoonful of honey or sugar. A great afternoon snack.

English Muffin Pizza

Split muffins in half and toast. Add tomato sauce (or catsup), a slice of cheese and some salami or ground beef. Bake in 350° oven until cheese is melted.

Buckley, Helen E. **Grandfather and I.** New York: Lothrop, Lee & Shepard, 1959.

> A small boy enjoys walking and exploring with his grandfather who is never in a hurry.

Buckley, Helen E. **My Sister and I.** New York: Lothrop, Lee & Shepard, 1963.

> The importance of relationships as experienced by sisters in early childhood is stressed in rhyme.

Cohen, Miriam. **Will I Have a Friend?** New York: Macmillan Publishing Co., 1967.

> Jim wants a friend the first day of school, but it takes until nap time to discover his first friend.

Hallinan, P.K. **We're Very Good Friends, My Brother and I.** Chicago, IL: Regensteiner Press, 1973.

> Written in rhyme, the close relationship between two brothers is explained.

Kramon, Florence. **Eugene and the New Baby.** Chicago, IL: Follett Publishing Co., 1967.

> Eugene has a new brother, and he and his father decide on an "acceptable" place to put the baby when mother brings him home.

Lenski, Lois. **The Little Family.** New York: Doubleday Publishing Co., 1932.

> The book tells about the daily routine of a typical day in the life of a very typical American family.

Slobodkin, Louis. **One Is Good, But Two Are Better.** New York: Vanguard Press, 1956.

> Written in rhyme, the advantages in playing games are definitely better when there are two people involved.

Zolotow, Charlotte. **Big Brother.** New York: Harper & Row, 1960.

> Big Brother teases Little Sister and makes her cry until she finds a way to make him stop teasing and be her friend.

Zolotow, Charlotte. **Big Sister and Little Sister.** New York: Harper & Row, 1966.

> The story of two sisters who look after each other and help each other.

Draw a big ball for the big boy.
Draw a little ball for the little boy.
Color the picture.

NOTES

FIVE SENSES

--- **Vocabulary** ---

Hear, see, taste, touch, smell, high, low, rough, smooth, humor, soft, furry, sticky, salty, bitter, dry, sour, sweet.

Seeing Objects

Isolating the sense of sight makes the child aware of what seeing means. Gather a variety of objects and place them on a tray. Allow each child to choose an object. Hold the object in front of the child's face and say, "You see a ball." Now cover the child's eyes with your hand and say, "You do not see a ball." Do this with all the children, emphasizing that eyes are for seeing. Use vocabulary: see, do not see.

What's Missing?

Place four different fruits, small toys or alphabet blocks on a tray. Play a game by having the children close their eyes and then remove an item. Let the children take turns guessing the missing item.

Describing Objects

Describe an object in the room by shape, color or size. Ask the children to guess the object you are thinking about. Encourage the children to try to describe the object and let the other children try to guess what it is.

Look in a Mirror

Have the children look at their eyes in a mirror. Ask, "What can you learn about your eyes?" Shine a bright light into someone's eyes. Watch the iris and pupil. What is happening to them? Have the children close their eyes for several minutes and then open them. Observe what happens. Have the children describe what happens to their eyes. Count the number of times a person blinks in one minute.

Guess the Sound

Record various sounds, such as an eggbeater, siren, telephone ring, dripping water, doorbell, a crying baby, piano, a dog barking, a car starting, a knock at the door or an alarm clock. Listen to the tape and see if the children can identify the different sounds.

L A N G U A G E

continued

Bottle Scales

Make a bottle scale with the children by filling soda bottles with different levels of colored water. Use a bottle capper so that the bottles can be transported without spilling. A bottle with more water in it makes a higher sound than one with less water. Use a drumstick or pencil for striking the bottles. Strike one bottle, and ask a child to strike another bottle with a sound **higher** or **lower** than the tone yours produced. Which bottle in the group makes the **highest** sound? Which bottle makes the **lowest** sound? Use vocabulary: high, higher, highest; low, lower, lowest. This also makes a new and simple instrument for the children to enjoy when they have free time.

Identifying Sounds

Give children an opportunity to identify sounds in terms of high and low. Using a tape recorder as a stimulus, ask the children if they would like to record sounds they make with their voices. Demonstrate first and play back. Example: "grumble, grumble" (low)—"screech" (high). Encourage the children to make sounds and discuss whether each is high or low. Then listen to the tape.

Lunch Bag Mystery

Have several lunch-sized paper bags available. Put a familiar object in each one (example: ball, pencil, pipe cleaner or a block). Fold over the top and staple securely. Rattle the bags and ask the children if they can guess what is in the bags. Let the children hold the bags to the light and look at the shadow. Shake the bag; feel it. After guessing, tear open the bags to verify.

Variation: Collect a variety of fruits and vegetables and put them in a paper bag. Blindfold one child, and give her one of the foods to see if she can identify it by touch. You may also want to have a tray with several pieces of fruit and vegetables on it. Name one, and see if the child can find it. This exercise develops tactile sensitivity.

Feel Box

Make a "Feel Box." Fill a box with various objects and then ask the child to put her hand inside an opening. Ask, "Can you guess what is inside just by feeling it?" Describe what you feel and see if someone can guess what it is. Have the children feel the various objects and tell how they feel—soft, cold, smooth, furry, rough, sticky.

Variation I: Put an assortment of hard and soft objects in the box. Give each child a turn at pulling out a soft object and then a hard object. Next, allow each child to pull any object from the box. The child must then state whether the object is hard or soft. In this way she is also verbalizing the concept.

Variation II: Gather a variety of objects that are both hard and soft to develop tactile awareness. Present each item, and allow each child to handle it and pass it on. Use objects which have both a hard and soft part, such as a pencil, paintbrush, chalk eraser, shirt with buttons or a feather. This is a comparative activity and develops a discriminatory awareness of hard and soft relative to the situation. Have the children show what part of the item is soft and what part is hard.

Smelling Odors

Isolating the sense of smell makes a child aware of what smelling means. We smell through our noses; noses are for smelling. Explain that by drawing in more air (sniffing) you intensify smell. On a tray, have a variety of things to smell, such as spices, herbs, menthol, perfume and flowers. The odors need not be familiar to the children. Give everyone a turn at smelling. Exaggerate by sniffing.

continued

Picture Smells

Look at pictures of things that have smells. Describe what the smells would be like if the pictures were real.

Familiar Smells

Have the children close their eyes tightly. Have a variety of familiar objects with smells on a covered tray, such as soap, perfume, pepper, cinnamon, flower, coffee, lemon or extract flavors dabbed on cotton balls. Place each item under the child's nose and ask her to identify it.

LANGUAGE
continued

Tasting Experience

Much of what we think is taste is really smell. Pinch your nose closed and eat a cracker. Ask the children if it tastes the same as when they don't hold their noses.

Place salt, sugar, baking soda, lemon juice, honey, mustard, flour, vinegar and vanilla in separate cups for the children to taste. Ask the children to tell you if each tastes salty, bitter, dry, sour or sweet.

Variation: Look in a mirror and observe the bumps on the surface of the tongue. The sensation of taste is located in a cluster of cells called taste buds that are spread unevenly over the tongue. The taste buds can recognize only four stimuli: sweet, sour, salty and bitter. Taste buds at the tip of the tongue are sensitive to sweetness and saltiness. Along the sides, the buds are sensitive to sourness, and in the back, bitterness. Many foods have more than one taste. Using a medicine dropper, put different substances—water, vinegar, salt, sugar and mixed cocoa and water—on different parts of the children's tongues. Rinse the mouths after each substance. Have the children tell you which area of the tongue told them what the substance was.

Counting Pegs

Counting pegs in boards or tile are an important piece of equipment in a preschool. Give each child a pile of pegs and a board in which to insert them. Tell the child that when the holes are full, there will be one hundred pegs on the board. Call it a "Birthday Cake," and when the board is full, sing "Happy Birthday" to the child and let her blow out the imaginary candles.

Clapping Numbers

Play a game of clapping numbers with the children. Lay out large cards with numbers printed on them face down. Each child takes a turn at turning over a number and showing it to the group. Then everyone claps the number on the card. Be sure to include zero (no clap).

Sense of Humor

Point out to the children that there is another sense we all have—the "sense" of humor. What one person finds funny another will not. Invite the children to join you in a "laughing circle." Sit on the floor in a group with yourself in the center. Make faces, gestures and noises to make the children laugh. Suggest that someone replace you in the center. Ask, "Can you make us laugh?" Children enjoy "clowning around," and this is a fun way for them to express themselves. It also builds confidence because one child is drawing a reaction from the whole group (and most children will laugh readily in this situation).

Float and Sink

Put ice cubes in a glass. Tell the class that you are going to cover the ice cubes with water. Pour water into the glass. The ice cubes won't stay under water. They float on top. Why? Ice cubes float on water because they are lighter than water. Have a bowl of water available along with various objects, such as a crayon, block, nail, scissors, ball, leaf, paper clip, straw, pencil, cork, marble or balloon. Have students predict if the object will float or sink. Place items in two categories—"sink" or "swim." Provide other objects for individual discovery and classification.

Water Music

Through water play, children can visualize how sound can travel. Prepare five large water glasses or bowls by pouring different levels of water into each one. Place glasses or bowls on folded towels, rubber mats or a thick stack of folded newspaper. Have the children strike the edge of the glass or bowl with a soft mallet or wooden spoon. Stir the water gently with a finger and listen to the lovely bell-tone sound and its echo.

Variation: Fill a large bowl or pan with water. Strike triangles, tuning forks or large nails hanging from string. Immediately lower each item into the water without touching the edge of the container. Listen to the sound that results. Add drops of food coloring to the water and repeat the sound producing experiment. You can now **see** as well as hear sound traveling through water.

——————— **Toe Pictures** ———————

Want a good, ticklish time? Have the children take off their shoes and draw faces on their toes with ball-point pens. It tickles! And toes make the funniest heads you've ever seen.

Painting

Tempera Activities: Tempera paint is inexpensive and provides many different art experiences for children. The paint should not be diluted so much that it becomes too pallid and watery. Juice cans make ideal containers for each color. When mixing the paint, add two tablespoons laundry detergent. The detergent aids in the removal of the paint from clothes in the event of an accident.

Although easels are fun to use when painting, here are additional ways in which tempera paint can be used:

Ink Blots: Prefold paper and drop thick paint onto the open sheet from a tongue depressor or brush. Refold and open again. Several colors may be used.

Wet Paper: Wet the paper with a sponge and then drop on paint with a brush. Watch the drops spread into designs.

String Painting: Dip short lengths of string into bowls of paint, drip the paint from the string on the paper and remove. Or, fold the paper and then pull the string out while the paper is held shut with one hand.

Block Painting: Dip objects into bowls of paint and then press or run the objects on paper. The objects may be spools, corks, sink stoppers, sponges, jar lids, small blocks, small cars, scrub brushes, potatoes cut into shapes or bottle caps.

Dry-powder Painting: Put dry-powder tempera paint in dishes. Paint with wads of cotton to give a soft effect.

Textured Paint: Mix textured substances with the paints for different effects, adding a little glue to ensure sticking. Some suggestions for substances: salt, sand, fine sawdust, coffee grounds, cornmeal, rock salt.

Roll Painting: Fill roll-on deodorant bottles with tempera paint (a thinner solution than used on an easel) and let the children roll them on the paper.

Squeeze Bottles: Put paint in a squeeze bottle and add a little liquid starch to prevent the paint from spilling out too quickly. Now, hold the bottle above the paper and squeeze. Raise and lower the bottle to change the size of the paint drips. Try different bottles and colors. Place the tip of the bottle directly on the paper and move it around to make all kinds of lines.

ART
continued

Straw Painting: Drop paint onto paper. Then produce designs by blowing through drinking straws where the paint drops.

Foot Painting: If you feel ambitious, mix up some paint, set the paper on the ground outside and let the children paint with their feet.

Sponge Painting: Dip pieces of sponge into paint and then dab on white or colored paper.

───────────────── Snacks ─────────────────

Different types of bread make interesting snacks and cooking experiences. Try different varieties, such as rye, pumpernickel, wheat, buttermilk, egg bread, white, French, Italian, raisin or different grain breads. Bread can be toasted or eaten as is.

Try the different breads with various toppings.

- butter and jam
- cinnamon
- apple butter

- peanut butter
- honey
- melted cheese

COOK

TO LEARN

Brown, Margaret Wise. **Country Noisy Book.** New York: Harper & Row, 1940.
> Muffin is placed in a box and put on the train when the family goes to the country, and discovers many different noises on the train and in the country.

Brown, Margaret Wise. **Indoor Noisy Book.** New York: Harper & Row, 1942.
> Muffin gets a cold and while resting, hears all sorts of noises inside and outside the house.

Brown, Margaret Wise. **The Quiet Noisy Book.** New York: Harper & Row, 1950.
> Muffin wakes up and hears a very soft noise and tries to guess what it is.

Brown, Margaret Wise. **Summer Noisy Book.** New York: Harper & Row, 1951.
> On a car trip to the country, Muffin hears different noises in the country and on the farm.

Brown, Margaret Wise. **Winter Noisy Book.** New York: Harper & Row, 1947.
> Muffin watches the leaves fall off the tree one day and then hears an unusual sound outside. After much guessing, Muffin discovers it is snow.

Garelick, May. **Sound of a Summer Night.** New York: Young Scott, 1963.
> The author describes the sounds and moods of summer evening, night and morning in rhyme.

Perkins, Al. **The Ear Book.** New York: Random House, 1968.
> A boy and his dog hear various noises through the course of the day.

Showers, Paul. **Find Out By Touching.** New York: Thomas Y. Crowell, 1961.
> An explanation of how different objects feel and various guessing games to play that involve touching.

Showers, Paul. **The Listening Walk.** New York: Thomas Y. Crowell, 1961.
> A boy, his father and their dog take a walk and enjoy listening to all the different sounds in their neighborhood.

Talk with a friend about one of these pictures.
How would it smell, feel, taste, look, sound?
Color the other pictures.

NOTES

WEATHER

—————— **Vocabulary** ——————

Hot, cold, thermometer, mercury, before, after, rain, clouds, wind, fog, storm, mist, drizzle, in front of, in back of.

Observing Weather

Observe the weather outside. Ask the children what words describe the weather. Can they tell the difference between rain, snow, sleet, fog, mist, drizzle, thunder, lightning, a blizzard or a hurricane? These are not words or concepts to be taught in isolated ways, but things to be observed and talked about as they happen.

Thermometer

Using a room thermometer, show the children the line of mercury. When it goes **up**, it's hotter. When it goes **down**, it's colder. Put one thermometer in a cup of crushed ice (ice is cold). Watch the mercury go down. Put another thermometer in a cup of hot water and watch the mercury go up. Keep a thermometer in the room and check it daily. Use the terms—thermometer, mercury, hot and cold when referring to the temperature.

Variation: Put a thermometer in the hot sun and another in the shade. Note the difference in the mercury column. Take a thermometer from a refrigerator and place it near a stove. Note the rise in temperature. Let the children try to explain the change.

Clothes for Different Weather

Collect a variety of pictures of clothing which can be worn in different climates. Label meat trays "hot" and "cold" for sorting. Put a drawing of a sun on one and a drawing of a snowman on the other. Encourage the children to assist you in sorting the clothing pictures by putting those articles of clothing you would wear in hot weather with the sun, and those you would wear in a cold climate with the snowman. You may wish to make a "hot and cold" poster with the pictures.

LANGUAGE

continued

Hot and Cold

Discuss hot and cold by setting up silly hypothetical situations in which the children guess whether you would be **hot** or **cold.** Example: "I am sitting near an open oven. I would be _____?"; "I am wearing a fur coat on the beach. I would be _____?"; "I am wearing a bikini in the snow. I would be _____?" This is a verbal game and encourages abstract application of the concepts of hot and cold.

Before …

… After

Before and After

Understanding the concepts of **before** and **after** is essential to telling time. Demonstrate these concepts without defining them by setting up several **before** and **after** situations.

1. Hold up an egg and say, "before." Drop it into a bowl and say, "after."
2. Stand a block on end and say, "before." Knock it over and say, "after."
3. Hold up a piece of paper and say, "before." Crumple it and say, "after."

It is important to use only the terms **before** and **after** during the demonstration. Have a variety of materials available and encourage each child in turn to play the "Before and After" game. These concepts are also important in developing observation skills.

Variation: Use magnetic letters and board to play "Before and After." Put up one letter on the middle of the board. Place another to the left of it and say, "before." Then, place a letter to the right of it and say, "after." Encourage the children to put up the **before** and **after** letters. Use the phrases **in front of** and **in back of** to describe positions of before and after. After the children are able to follow a directive in arranging the letters, change the activity so that you are setting up the situation and the children verbalize **before** and **after.**

Adding Machine / Calculator

Borrow an adding machine from a friend. Let the children experiment by punching numbers into the machine and seeing them come out on the tape. Some of the children may want to count to ten on the machine, while others will just enjoy pushing the buttons. Explain that businesses use adding machines to add numbers that are important to them. Explain that soon many of the children will be learning how to add. A hand calculator can also be used to illustrate different styles of adding.

Counting from One to Ten

This activity encourages an understanding of a one to one (numerical unit) relationship in counting. Begin the activity by encouraging a discussion of what one could build with ten blocks. When ideas have been thrown out, count out ten blocks by using this verse:

One, two blocks for you
Three, four here are more
Five, six do some tricks
Seven, eight let's not wait
Nine, ten do it again
We can count from **one** to **ten.**

Be sure to handle each block as you count its number. Now, build a simple structure. "What could it be?" Ask the children if they would like to build with ten cuisenaire rods. Count out ten rods with each child using the verse. Encourage building and counting, always handling each rod as you say its number.

Variation: Continue the "one for" counting verse while counting beans into jars. Each child is given a small jar (baby food jar is fine) and ten beans. A glass jar is better than a paper cup, since the child can visualize what he has already counted. Begin with all ten beans in the lid, and remove them one at a time by placing them into the jar. Sing the counting verse while placing your beans. Do this as a group activity so that the children can handle the beans "one for one."

Number Hopscotch

Children retain what they learn when they experience it. In order to bodily experience number meaning, play a game of number hopscotch. The children take turns at tossing a bean bag into numbered squares. The number of the square in which the bag lands signifies the number of steps they may take from a starting line toward a finish line. (Establish the lines on the floor beforehand with chalk.) When a child's turn comes up, he'll have to mark his position before moving. A block labeled with his name serves well. The game may end when one child reaches the finish line.

─────────────── **Rainbow / Prism** ───────────────

Make a rainbow with a prism. Take a glass prism outside in the sun and let the children shine the rainbow on walls and floors. A stream of water sprayed from a hose in the sunlight at the right angle will also make a rainbow.

Air

Ask the children where air is. Can they see it? Can they feel it? Can they hear it? Explain that air is everywhere. It is all around them. They can feel it when they put their arms straight out and whirl them around. Give each child a drinking straw. Have the children blow through the straws onto their hands. Next, blow through the straws into a glass of water. Ask the children if they feel air and if they can see air. Give the children balloons. Blow them up and let them drop. Ask the children what pushed the balloon down and around and around. Place an empty pop bottle into a big bowl of water. Watch the bubbles surface. Ask the class where the bubbles came from. Have students answer these questions. "Where is air? Can you see air? Can you feel air?"

─────────────── **Rainy Day Song** ───────────────
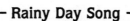

The children know that rain is very important to help plants grow and to renew the supply of drinking water. However, it sometimes ruins plans to go on a picnic or to play outdoors. Teach the children this Rainy Day Song and let them make up new verses to go with whatever they are doing in the room that day.

"Rainy Day Song"
(Sung to the tune of "Mary Had a Little Lamb")

"What shall we do on a rainy day, rainy day, rainy day?
What shall we do on a rainy day, when we can't go out to play?

We'll clean the room on a rainy day, rainy day, rainy day.
We'll clean the room on a rainy day when we can't go out to play.

We'll make some toast on a rainy day, rainy day, rainy day,
We'll make some toast on a rainy day when we can't go out to play."

Pretending

Pantomime the following actions:
1. You are a flower—start as a seed, grow up and blossom.
2. You are blowing up a balloon until it pops!
3. You are a snowman melting in the hot sun.
4. You are watching a game and it starts to rain.
5. You are ice skating and you fall down.
6. You are barefoot and walk on the hot sidewalk in the summertime.
7. You are eating a drippy ice-cream cone.
8. You step on a piece of bubble gum and it sticks to your shoe.
9. You walk into a very hot room.
10. You walk into a very cold room.

Badminton

An old nylon stocking stretched over a rounded coat hanger makes an excellent badminton racket. Use a ball of nylon net and make a court with chalk on the playground. A fun game!!

Snowflakes

Snowflakes in summer? Yes! Colored tissue paper and scissors are the ingredients. Fold the paper and cut out small notches. Open them up and you will have summer snowflakes. Hang them from light fixtures to dance in the summer breeze.

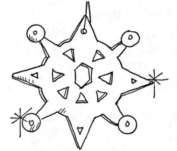

Washing the World

Discuss daily hygiene—baths and showers—and what they do for us. Ask, "Did you know that the world is washed too?" Relate this idea to nature and to storms. Explain that lightning makes a hole in the air. When the air rushes in to fill the hole, it makes a loud noise. Put on a stormy record and bodily express rain, wind, thunder and lightning.

COOK

TO LEARN

Rice Krispies Cookies

marshmallows or marshmallow cream (16 ounces)
1 stick margarine
3 cups Rice Krispies

Melt margarine and marshmallows. Add cereal. Put into a greased 11 x 13 inch pan. Mash down or shape into balls or other shapes. Grease hands slightly before handling, and put finished cookies on waxed paper.

Banana Wheat Germ Treats

Slice bananas. Roll in a mixture of half milk and half honey. Place the slices in a plastic bag of wheat germ and shake until coated. Can be refrigerated until time to eat.

Crunchy Peanut Butter Bread

2 cups flour
⅓ cup sugar
2 teaspoons baking powder
1 teaspoon salt
¾ cup peanut butter
½ cup peanuts chopped
1 cup milk
1 egg

Mix dry ingredients together in a bowl. Add peanut butter and blend with a fork. Thoroughly mix egg and milk together. Stir into dry ingredients and peanut butter. Add chopped peanuts. Mix until just blended. Pour into greased loaf pan. Bake at 350° for about 50 minutes. Makes one loaf.

Early Morning Smoothie

1 banana
1 egg
1 cup milk
1 teaspoon vanilla
¼ cup apple or pineapple juice

Mash the banana in a mixing bowl. Add beaten egg, milk, vanilla and juice. Mix well until smooth. Pour in a tall glass for an early energy boost. Can be mixed in a blender.

Barr, Jene, and Chapin, Cynthia. **What Will the Weather Be?** Chicago: Albert Whitman and Co., 1965.
Explains the various instruments used to predict the weather.

Fisher, Aileen. **I Like Weather.** New York: Thomas Y. Crowell, 1963.
Written in rhyme, a boy and his dog enjoy the various activities that each season provides.

Hall, Malcolm. **Forecast.** New York: Coward, McCann & Geoghegan, Inc., 1977.
Caroline Porcupine has to prove that she can handle the job as a weather reporter for the Claws and Paws newspaper.

Hall, Marie. **Gilberto and the Wind.** New York: The Viking Press, 1963.
A small, lonely Mexican boy finds that the wind makes a fascinating playmate.

Hutchins, Pat. **The Wind Blew.** New York: Macmillan Publishing Co., 1974.
A story written in rhyme describing how a stiff wind carries away different objects in its path.

Shaw, Charles G. **It Looked Like Spilt Milk.** New York: Harper & Row, 1947.
White blobs appear on deep blue pages and clues are given, but the identity is kept secret until the end.

Tressett, Alvin. **Follow the Wind.** New York: Lothrop, Lee & Shepard, 1950.
A noisy wind affects many objects, but at last it becomes sleepy and quiet.

Wiest, Claire and Robert. **Down the River Without a Paddle.** Childrens Press, 1973.
A caterpillar, blown by a storm, makes a harrowing trip down the river on a leaf barely escaping with his life.

Wolff, Barbara. **Evening Gray, Morning Red.** New York: Macmillan Publishing Co., 1976.
A handbook of weather forecasting based on rhymes, sayings and signs used in America for centuries.

Zolotov, Charlotte. **The Storm Book.** New York: Harper & Row, 1952.
A small boy and his mother watch a summer storm and describe its beauty.

Draw dot to dot to finish the snowy day picture.

Read this nursery rhyme that tells about the weather.
Draw a picture to illustrate the rhyme.

It's raining, it's pouring,
The old man is snoring.
He went to bed with a cold in his head
And he didn't wake up until morning.

NOTES

NIGHT AND DAY

---------- **Vocabulary** ----------

Silhouette, profile, stars, moon, midnight, noon, time, morning, evening.

Homonyms

These are words that sound alike but have different meanings. These word games are for older children. Younger children do not grasp language as a thing in itself. Older children however, should enjoy playing games with language. Explain to the children that two words can sound the same but mean two different things. Example: Use pictures to illustrate these pairs of words:

bare—bear
pear—pair
flour—flower
hear—here
not—knot
son—sun

Riddles

Use riddles to increase the child's ability to solve problems. Examples:

I come from the sky.
I come in drops.
I wash houses.
I wash trees.
I help make things grow.
I feed rivers.
I fall on umbrellas.
What am I? (rain)

I am in the sky.
I help makes things grow.
I put color in the flowers.
I am bright.
I am hot.
I shine in the daytime.
People like me.
What am I? (sun)

I grow on a plant.
I am hard.
Sometimes I am hot.
I go pop, pop, pop.
Then I am white.
Boys like me.
Girls like me.
What am I? (popcorn)

I am yellow.
I am made from milk.
Sometimes I am soft.
Sometimes I am hard.
I am good to eat.
I am put on bread.
What am I? (butter)

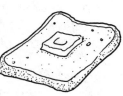

45

I am good to eat.
Boys like me in the summer.
Girls like me in the summer.
I am made of cream.
I am made with ice.
I am cold.
What am I? (ice cream)

I am white.
I have a shell.
My shell may break.
People like me.
I am good to eat.
The hen lays me.
What am I? (egg)

I make noise.
You can hear me.
You cannot see me.
I make sailboats go.
What am I? (wind)

I come from the sky.
I am white.
I am cold.
I fall softly.
What am I? (snow)

I am round.
I am red.
I am juicy.
I grow on a tree.
I am good to eat.
What am I? (apple)

I can fly.
I make honey.
I say, "buzz, buzz."
What am I? (bee)

Shadows

To understand the effect of light casting a shadow, talk with the children about the shadows they have seen and how they felt about them. What made the shadows? With the room darkened, use a flashlight as a light source (other light sources may be lamps or the sun) and shine it on an object. Is the shadow cast? Where? Behind the object? What does it look like? Emphasize the fact that in order to create a shadow, you must have a light source.

Silhouette

continued

Shadows are outline objects. Tell the children that you can draw the outline of their faces by tracing their shadows. Use the film projector for a light source, and explain that you must shine the light source on their heads in order to create a shadow behind them. Mount paper on the wall and trace the children's shadows. Then, give the children crayons to color in their shadows.

Variation: Put objects such as a ball, feather or hammer in front of a lamp. Draw the object's profile and cut it out. See if the children can recognize the silhouette.

Pairs

A pair is made up of two corresponding things that go together (a pair of shoes, a pair of hands, a pair of eyes). Cut pictures from a magazine and paste them on 3 x 5 inch cards. A discussion of the pairs is begun by asking, "Who is wearing two shoes that are alike?" It should be pointed out that each child has a pair of shoes. Ask them to find other pairs of things on their bodies or in the room. Now, play a game of matching pairs with the 3 x 5 inch cards. Have available two trays, one for pairs, one for non-pairs. Afford each child the opportunity to turn over the top card and identify the card as showing a pair or non-pair. Have the child place the card in the appropriate tray and state whether the card shows a pair or non-pair.

Pair Poster

Make a "pair poster" with the children. Use a large sheet of poster-board labeled "pairs." Have available pictures from magazines that depict pairs. Show each picture to the children and ask their assistance in finding pairs. After discussion of each picture, give one to a child to paste on the poster. Display the group poster on a bulletin board or individual posters can be made and taken home.

──────────────── **"Hickory, Dickory Dock"** ────────────────

FINGER

PLAY

"Hickory, dickory, dock. (rest elbow in the palm of the other hand and swing upraised arm back and forth)

The mouse ran up the clock. (creep fingers up arm to the palm of the other hand)

The clock struck one. (clap hands)

The mouse ran down. (creep fingers down to elbow)

Hickory, dickory, dock." (swing arm as before)

"Two Little Hands"

"Two little hands go clap, clap, clap.
Two little feet go tap, tap, tap.
Two little hands go thump, thump, thump.
Two little feet go jump, jump, jump.
One little child turns slowly around.
One little child sits (quietly, carefully, slowly) down."

Measuring

Get two jars, one tall and slender, one short and wide. Fill each with an equal number of beans. Then, ask the children to guess which container has more. They will probably choose the tall, slender jar. Then measure the beans with a measuring cup. Explain that taller does not necessarily mean more. The shape of the container can influence how "high" the beans go. Let the children experiment with various containers, each time measuring the beans with a measuring cup to be sure the portions are equal.

Full and Empty

In this activity, the children have graduated from pouring a solid to pouring a liquid. Give each child a milk carton with water in it and a paper cup. Demonstrate by filling the cup and saying "full." Then, pour the water back into the carton and say "empty." Do this activity outside where children are not frustrated by spills. They love it!

Night and Day

Cut out items that are used in daylight and paste onto pieces of flannel. (Examples: sunglasses, beach umbrella, suntan lotion, shovel and pail, hat). Do the same for pictures of things that are used only at night. (Examples: flashlight, lamp, pajamas, hair curlers, car headlights). Have the children put items into the appropriate category—"day" or "night," and have them explain why the items belong in that category.

Perspective

Collect three or four large pictures from magazines or purchase them from a school supply store. Ask a child to point to an object in the picture which seems close by. Ask another child to point to an object in the picture which seems to be far away. Discuss how objects and people seem to get smaller as they move farther away.

Bowling

Old aluminum pop cans make ideal pins for an inexpensive bowling set. Clean them, set them up and use a volleyball for a bowling ball.

Sun Collage

Materials: blue construction paper, yellow construction paper, white cotton balls, glue.

Glue cotton balls onto blue construction paper to form clouds. Cut out a circle of yellow for the sun and glue it on the paper.

Night Collage

Materials: black construction paper, stars, white tempera paint, small sponge squares.

Dab white paint on black construction paper with the sponge. After the paint dries, have the children lick and stick stars on the picture to imitate the nighttime sky.

Photo Imprints

Materials: light sensitive paper (can be purchased from a science supply warehouse).

Give each child a photo sensitive sheet of paper. Have the child put objects on top of the paper such as leaves, seashells, a ring or silverware. Take the paper with the objects on top of it and place it in the sunlight for 45 minutes. Remove the objects and their shadows remain.

You Are My Sunshine

Buy some inexpensive paper plates. Let the children color them with "sun colors." Pass out scissors and let the children cut slits about 1 inch deep around the whole edge. The teacher can then cut two eye holes and glue the paper plate sun onto a wooden tongue depressor. Held in front of the face, it becomes a sun mask. Teach the children to sing "You Are My Sunshine" while holding the masks up.

Twinkle, Twinkle

The paper plate mask can be adapted for a nighttime song, too. The teacher can cut the paper plate into a five-pointed star. After attaching the tongue depressor, the plates can be passed out to the children. Glitter, sequins or other goodies can be glued on to make a pretty star. "Twinkle, Twinkle, Little Star" is the theme song for this activity.

COOK

TO LEARN

——————————————— Applesauce ———————————————

6 apples
3 to 4 tablespoons honey
1½ cups water
1 teaspoon cinnamon

Peel, core and slice apples. Cook in water in a covered pan until tender (about 30 minutes). After apples are tender, either mash the apples with a potato masher and add honey and cinnamon to taste, or use a food mill or sieve to purée the apples.

Variation: Cook the apples without peeling. If using red apples, you will get pink applesauce.

Serve sections of apples on toothpicks. Make a fondue mixture of peanut butter, marshmallow cream, honey and coconut and/or honey and granola.

Apple Crisp

1 can (22 oz.) apple pie filling
1 cup quick cooking oats
½ cup butter or margarine, softened
½ cup firmly packed brown sugar
¼ cup flour
1 teaspoon cinnamon
½ teaspoon nutmeg

Heat oven to 325°. Spread apple filling in an 8 x 8 inch baking pan. In a bowl, combine the remaining ingredients and mix well. Spread over apples. Bake 25-30 minutes. Makes 6 one-half cup servings.
Top with vanilla ice cream if desired.

Apple Frypan Pudding

6 cups sliced apples
2 tablespoons lemon juice
2 tablespoons sugar
1 cup brown sugar

2 teaspoons cinnamon
1 teaspoon nutmeg
2 cups finely crushed graham crackers
1 cube margarine

Brush pan with margarine. Arrange apple slices on bottom of pan. Sprinkle with lemon juice and sugar. Stir brown sugar, cracker crumbs, spices and melted margarine together with fork. Spread over apples and cook 20 minutes at 320°.

De Regniers, Beatrice. **The Shadow Book.** New York: Harcourt Brace Jovanovich, 1960.
> Photographs with captions describe a child and his shadow at play.

Duvoisin, Roger. **Day and Night.** New York: Knopf, 1960.
> A poodle named Day meets an owl named Night and they become friends, talking to each other with barks and hoots late into the night to the distress of the Pennyfeathers.

Ginsburg, Mirra. **Where Does the Sun Go At Night?** New York: Greenwillow Books, 1981.
> Pictures accompany the questions and answers as to where the sun goes at night and what it does there.

Scheck, Eleanor. **One Summer Night.** New York: Greenwillow Books, 1977.
> Laura plays a record on a hot summer night which causes those that hear it to sing, play musical instruments and dance in the street.

Schlein, Miriam. **Here Comes Night.** Racine, WI: Whitman Publishing Co., 1957.
> It is dusk and the sun sets, telling the farm, the sea, the city and the people that it is time to rest and sleep.

Schneider, Nina. **While Susie Sleeps.** New York: Young Scott, 1948.
> When Susie sleeps at night, many activities continue, from animals moving about to bakers, truckers, milkmen and printers getting their products ready for the morning delivery.

Tressett, Alvin. **Sun Up.** New York: Lothrop, Lee & Shepard, 1949.
> A hot summer day on the farm begins with a crowing rooster and continues to be very hot for everyone until a late afternoon storm brings coolness to all.

Tressett, Alvin. **Wake Up, City.** New York: Lothrop, Lee & Shepard, 1956.
> A city awakens with different activities.

Tressett, Alvin. **Wake Up, Farm.** New York: Lothrop, Lee & Shepard, 1955.
> The farm animals awake and announce dawn to the farmer and his family.

Zolotow, Charlotte. **Sleepy Books.** New York: Lothrop, Lee & Shepard, 1958.
> A story, beautifully illustrated in shades of blue, tells how children and different animals go to sleep.

Zolotow, Charlotte. **The Summer Night.** New York: Harper & Row, 1974.
> A little girl can't sleep at night and goes to her father who, together with her, enjoys the night's sights and sounds until she is ready to go to sleep.

Cut and paste the pictures in the correct box.

DAY

NIGHT

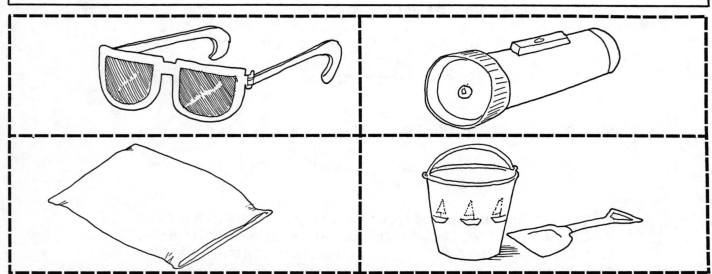

52

Here is a picture of something I like to do during the day.

Here is a picture of something I like to do at night.

COMMUNITY HELPERS

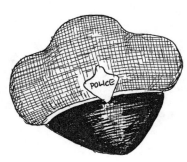

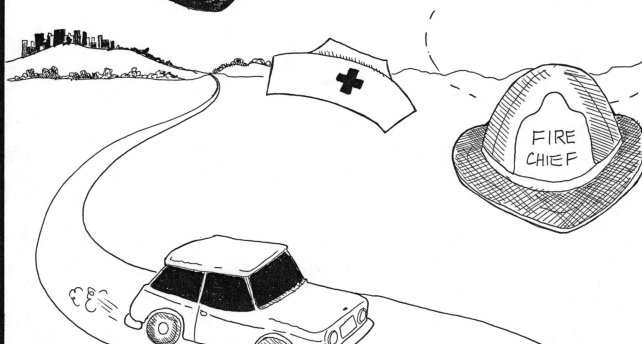

TRANSPORTATION

NOTES

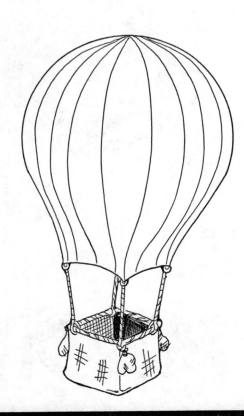

COMMUNITY HELPERS/ TRANSPORTATION

Vocabulary

Community, policeman, fireman, paramedic, mail carrier, mayor, garbage man, airport, bus terminal, fuel, bow, stern, automobile, vehicle, flashlight, jack, maps, airplane, transport.

Skyscrapers

Skyscrapers are very tall buildings. People live, work and play in them. Discuss skyscrapers with the children. Show pictures from books or magazines. Discuss what the people could be doing in each building. Talk about elevators and escalators. If possible, visit a city on a field trip and look at the skyscrapers. Perhaps you will see one under construction.

Build a Skyscraper

Using the classroom blocks, build as tall a structure as you can. You will have to sit on the floor. Let the children help you build one and then let them separate and build their own, either alone or in groups.

Cardboard Town

Collect small cardboard boxes. The ones foods and small gifts come in are best. Set aside one area for the town. Discuss with the children the things a town should have—fire station, grocery store, school. You may want to paint the boxes or cover them with construction paper. To make a skyscraper, glue boxes together before standing them upright. With a few small cars and pipe-cleaner people, the town is complete.

Sending Letters

Sending letters helps the children understand the need for a postal service. Begin by having the children "write" letters or draw pictures for their friends. Put these letters in envelopes and let the children deliver them to their friends' lockers or cubby holes. Some of the older children may be able to write their friends' names on the front of the envelopes.

continued

Going to the Mailbox

Have each child's parent address an envelope to whomever the child wants a letter or picture sent (grandma, sister, aunt). Have the children draw very nice pictures. You may write their names at the bottom or some may be able to write their names themselves. Put the pictures into the pre-addressed envelopes and walk to the nearest mailbox to mail them. Don't forget to mention the necessity for stamps.

Rules

Rules are an important part of any social structure. Discuss the playground rules with the children. Ask the children questions. Why were the rules set up? What would happen if we threw away the rules? Do you have rules at home? What are they? Does your city have rules? Does the United States have rules? What are some of the rules your parents have to follow?

Asking Permission

Encourage the children to ask permission before taking something. Set up imaginary situations where children will role-play asking permission to have something or go somewhere. Be sure to have the children say, "May I go please?" Stress the difference between "may" and "can."

Transportation

Have a variety of pictures of vehicles of transportation available (or have a book of different vehicles). As the pictures are shown to the children, ask them:

How do they move?
How are all these vehicles alike?
What kind of materials are used in building these vehicles?
What is a recreational vehicle?
What are some parts that have to be replaced from time to time?
How many years does a car last?
What do you do with a car when it gets too old?
Why do you wax a car?
Why do cars have to have a license plate?
Where do you buy a car?
What kind of fuel do different vehicles use?

Variation: Have the children tell what items might be found in a car and why. Put pictures on a flannel board and have the class identify the items, tell why they are kept in a car and how they can help you. Examples: flashlight, jack, chain, tissues, maps, shovel, compass, CB radio, coins. Play a game by placing the pictures randomly on the flannel board, and having the children try to identify the objects.

Matching Sets

This activity encourages an understanding of "set" and one-to-one relationships without verbal definition. Say, "Now I am going to make a set of four objects to match your set." Use marbles, coins, pencils or other small objects. Set up other sets and see if the children can make corresponding sets.

Coffee Can Match

Take four coffee cans with plastic lids and punch one set of holes in each lid. One lid has four holes, one has three holes, and so on. Put a slit in each lid large enough for a 3 x 5 inch card to go into. On 3 x 5 inch cards, draw sets of objects numbering from one to four. Give the cards to the children, and have them match the number of objects on their cards to the holes in the can lids and put the cards in the correct cans.

Outside Matching

On the pavement outside, draw enough boxes with chalk for each child playing to have his own box. Using rocks, sticks or any found object, create a model for the child to duplicate. Remember to keep the numbers under ten.

Dominoes

Children who have mastered matching sets up to ten, will probably enjoy learning to play dominoes. The game is simple and reinforces the ideas found in set matching.

Switchboard Operator

Get a cardboard box from the supermarket and paint one of the sides with tempera paint. Mark three rows of dots on the painted side with a crayon or marker. Poke a hole through each dot with a nail or ice pick. Cut as many 1-foot lengths of string as there are holes in the top row of dots. Push one end through the hole and knot it on the back. Tie nails or golf tees onto the dangling ends of strings. Poke both ends of a yard-length of string through a hole in the bottom of a Styrofoam or paper cup. Knot the ends and hang the cup around the neck. Play operator by speaking into the cup and plugging the nails into the different holes. Earphones, earmuffs or a headset will complete the outfit of the telephone operator.

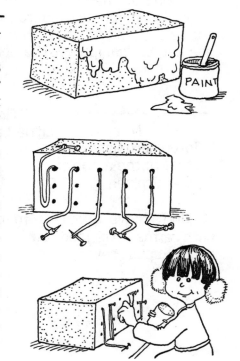

SKILLS

**LIFE
SKILLS**
continued

Dialing the Telephone

This is a good reinforcement for learning numbers and it is practical as well. Practice with a play phone. Demonstrate to the children how a phone is dialed and let them practice. Give them simple instructions like, "Please dial a five for me." Once the children have learned how to dial correctly, let them dial on a real phone and call for the time.

Hand Puppets

Children relate easily to puppets, dolls and stuffed toys, and often converse freely with them. Using a puppet is a good way to stimulate conversation. Use a watercolor marker to draw a face on your hand. Use the thumb and index finger as a mouth with the hand held in a loose fist. Draw eyes, eyebrows and ears, and add hair or glasses. Have each puppet assume the identity of one of the community helpers being studied in the unit. The helper could explain to the class what he does in the community to help people.

Walking Puppets

Draw or ditto community helper walking puppets onto sturdy oak tag. Color and cut them out. (You will have to cut out the puppets for younger children.) Cut two holes and stick two fingers through and "walk" the puppet on a table or floor.

Paper Bag Puppets

Have the children draw a face of some community helper on the bottom of a lunch-sized bag (white ones are best for this). Do not open the bag until the face is drawn. Then, tell them to carefully slip their hands in and use the natural fold in the bag to manipulate the head.

"Tiptoe Aeroplane"

(Sung to "Mary Had a Little Lamb")
"Tiptoe aeroplane, aeroplane, aeroplane,
Tiptoe, tiptoe aeroplane
Tiptoe airplane . . . STOP!"

Children move about room on tiptoes with arms extended until "STOP!" is sung. Repeat several times.

Stop 'n Go Signs

The crossing guard is a very important person in the community. Have the children make stop and go signs to use when playing with their trucks and cars. Use tongue depressors or craft sticks, red and green construction paper and glue. Pre-cut the octagon pieces of paper. Help the children write "stop" and "go" on the appropriate sides and glue to the sticks. Even if the children can't read, they will know that red means "stop" and green means "go."

Using Scissors

Give each child a pair of scissors. Show the children where the fingers go and how to make the blades open and close. Play a game of "open" and "close," having the children perform the correct action when you give the cue.

Cutting Fringe

This is an excellent way to develop those motor skills necessary in learning to write. Give each child a pair of scissors and a piece of paper. Demonstrate how to cut fringe, making sure not to cut all the way through the paper.

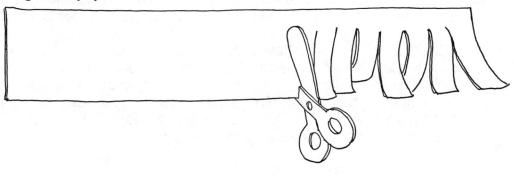

Cupcake Liner Flowers

Use colored paper liners for cupcakes for this activity. Cut from the outside edge to the center circle. Flatten out and use as flower petals. Glue to a piece of cardboard and add a stem and a few leaves with a crayon.

Car Carrier

Use a quart or a half-gallon milk carton. Rinse it out and cut off the top. Have the children cut out lots of pictures of cars, trucks, planes and boats from old magazines and glue them all over the milk carton as a collage. Punch two holes near the top edge on both sides of the carton. Attach yarn through the holes to make a handle for the carrier.

Variation: Get an empty ice-cream container from an ice-cream shop and make a carrier for the room.

continued

Racing Car

Paint a clothespin with tempera paint, either all one color or in a design. Cut four wheels from cardboard, oak tag or Styrofoam meat trays. Paint them black and glue them on. Draw or cut out a picture of a race-car driver and glue the picture to the appropriate space in the clothespin.

Clothespin Airplane

Have children paint an old-fashioned wooden clothespin a solid color. Draw stripes around the rounded end of the clothespin tip to represent the propeller section of the plane. Cut two rectangular shapes from oak tag or cardboard to represent wings for the body and tail of the plane. Poke two holes in the center of the wings so that the wings can be tied to the clothespin with either string or pipe cleaners. Use a pipe cleaner to tie the wings to the body and to form the landing gear by twisting the ends of the pipe cleaner into the wheels. Cut a piece of yellow construction paper into a propeller shape and glue it to the front of the plane.

Plastic Model Cars

Trace shapes (squares, rectangles, circles, triangles) on Styrofoam meat trays. Have students cut them out. Stick toothpicks into the foam pieces to build a model car. The pieces can be taken apart easily so another style of car can be made. Dipping the ends of the toothpick in glue will keep a model together permanently.

Box Boat

Collect empty boxes of different shapes and sizes. Empty toothpaste, soap, perfume and shaving boxes are great. Cut and fold the end of the largest one into a point to make the front of the boat. Paint the boxes with tempera paint. Glue different sizes of boxes together with the large one on the bottom. Cut two paper roll tubes at a slant at one end. Glue tubes to top of and back end of top box for smokestacks. Cut black construction paper into circles and glue on the boat to make portholes.

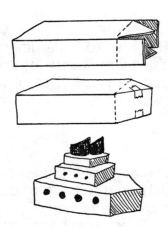

──────────────── **Easy Doughnuts** ────────────────

Packages of refrigerated biscuits

Open cans of biscuits and separate into individual pieces. Poke a hole in the center and stretch the biscuit out. Drop into hot grease and cook one minute on each side. Sprinkle doughnut with cinnamon sugar or powdered sugar.

Orange Shake

1 12-ounce can frozen orange juice concentrate
2 cups milk
2 cups water
4 tablespoons sugar
1 teaspoon vanilla
10-12 ice cubes

Place all ingredients in a blender. Cover and blend until smooth. Serve immediately. Serves 8-10. Other fruit juice concentrate can be substituted for orange juice.

COOK TO LEARN

──────────────── **Trips** ────────────────

A trip taken without preparation is rarely as successful or meaningful to the children as a well planned one. Discuss where you are going and what you are going to see. Sometimes you can even tell the children to be alert for specific things. Use appropriate pictures, books, stories, poems or songs for preparation. All the places they will visit are important to the community. Discuss how each plays a part in the life of a city. Think of some questions to ask the people you meet there.

Supermarket

As eager as young children are, they have a limited attention span, so do not try to do too much. Make several trips to the supermarket, each with a different focus. Watch the goods being delivered. Watch the boxes being unpacked and the merchandise being stamped. Look at all the different kinds of machines in the store.

Garage

Watch the gas being pumped into your car's tank. Watch the gas pump itself. What is happening? Try to see a car being raised with a hydraulic lift or a tire changed. Take the children with you when you have the oil and tires of your car checked. What kind of clothes do mechanics wear?

FIELD TRIPS

FIELD  continued

Policeman and Crossing Guard

Within walking distance of your house, there is probably an intersection or a school where a policeman or crossing guard is on duty. Watch what he does. How does he tell the vehicles and pedestrians to go? To stop? Children will enjoy talking to him and getting a good look at his uniform. The police station is of interest too; perhaps the desk sergeant on duty will spend a few minutes visiting with the children. He may show the children the inside of a police car, demonstrate the two-way radio and give a short safety speech.

Mailman

Make arrangements to meet your own mailman at your mailbox and then at the nearest pickup box on the corner to watch him gather the mail. Buy a stamp and mail a letter at the post office. Children are generally not allowed in the back of most post offices, but they can see a good deal if they look through the window at the parcel-post counter. Watch the packages being weighed and mailed.

Bus Driver

Sit near the driver of the bus. Watch what he does. Look at his uniform.

Fire Station

Some fire departments have open house days. If yours does not, make an appointment for a visit ahead of time. Do not insist that the children get on the equipment, even if they are invited to do so. Climbing on an engine can be a frightening experience for some preschoolers. Usually the children are invited to try on a fireman's hat, watch a fireman slide down the pole and inspect the engine thoroughly. Find out how the fire alarm works.

Airports

Watch airplanes taking off and landing. How do people get on and off a plane? How does a plane get its fuel? How does a plane appear to change in size as it goes farther away? How does a plane seem to change in size as it comes closer? Why is the sound it makes louder or softer?

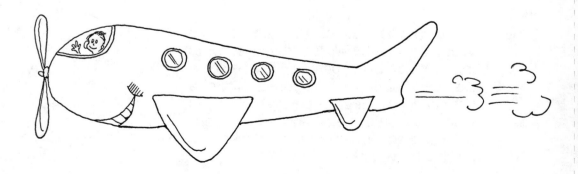

Burton, Virginia Lee. **Mike Mulligan and His Steam Shovel.** Boston, MA: Houghton Mifflin, 1939.

> Mike Mulligan and his steam shovel Mary Ann find a new place to call home when they find that steam shovels are being replaced by newer gasoline, electric and diesel motor shovels.

Cameron, Polly. **The Green Machine.** New York: Coward-McCann, 1969.

> A book of witty nonsense centering around a green car.

Dugan, William. **The Car Book.** New York: Golden Press, 1968.

> An explanation of all sorts of cars—taxis, police cars, race cars.

Graham, Margaret Bloy. **Benjy's Boat Trip.** New York: Harper & Row, 1977.

> A small dog takes a surprising boat trip and meets a ship's angry cat.

Lenski, Lois. **The Little Airplane.** Ithaca, NY: Walck & Rikhoff Bookpeddlers, 1938.

> Pilot Small explains how an airplane flies using accurate terms, and explains the basic parts of an airplane.

Lenski, Lois. **The Little Auto.** Ithaca, NY: Walck & Rikhoff Bookpeddlers, 1934.

> The story and pictures show Mr. Small taking care of his little red auto.

Lenski, Lois. **The Little Fire Engine.** Ithaca, NY: Walck & Rikhoff Bookpeddlers, 1946.

> A step by step picture of the work of a fireman from the sound of the alarm until the time the fire is out.

Lenski, Lois. **The Little Train.** Ithaca, NY: Walck & Rikhoff Bookpeddlers, 1940.

> Engineer Small takes very good care of his black, shiny train and all the important details of how the train operates are described.

Lenski, Lois. **Policeman Small.** Ithaca, NY: Walck & Rikhoff Bookpeddlers, 1962.

> A day in the life of a traffic policeman and how he helps everyone is shown in pictures in this book.

McPhail, David. **The Train.** Boston, MA: Little, Brown & Co., 1977.
Matthew's brother causes his train to crash to the floor. That night he can't sleep, and decides to repair the train so that passengers can continue their journey.

Piper, Watty. **Trucks.** New York: Platt and Munk, 1978.
An explanation of all sorts of trucks. Brightly illustrated.

Poulet, Virginia. **Blue Bug Safety Book.** Chicago, IL: Childrens Press, 1973.
Blue Bug obeys all safety signs in his path on his way home.

Shay, Arthur. **What Happens When You Mail a Letter?** Chicago, IL: Reilly & Lee, 1967.
Steven mails a letter and the letter is followed through the post office departments to its destination at his grandmother's house.

Woolley, Catherine. **I Like Trains.** New York: Harper & Row, 1944.
A little boy loves trains and through his eyes, all types of trains and their interiors are described.

Zion, Gene. **Dear Garbage Man.** New York: Harper & Row, 1957.
Stan saves the broken furniture and trash to give away instead of putting them in the chewer-upper, but a letter on the broken bed the next day causes him to change his mind about saving trash.

continued

Make an X on the things that help people get from one place to another.

NOTES

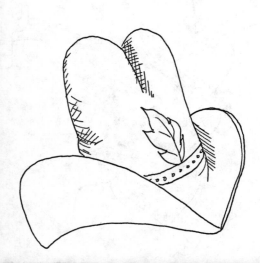

L'IL COWPOKES

Vocabulary

Cowboy, cowgirl, rodeo, ranch, chuck wagon, roundup, saddle, bridle, stirrup, branding iron, chaps.

Flannel Board

Using the pattern, cut out the various pieces of Cowboy Dan using colored felt. Set up the flannel board in front of the class. Read the poem "Cowboy Dan" to the children as you put him together on the board. You may want to stop and discuss the things a cowboy wears. Why does the cowboy wear chaps? Why does he wear boots instead of regular shoes? Why do cowboys prefer blue jeans to other kinds of pants? Then, take some of the felt pieces and pass each one to a member of the class. Reread the poem and let each child come to the flannel board and put up the article of clothing as it is mentioned in the poem. You may do this several times during the week, having different children put on different articles of clothing.

"Cowboy Dan"

Let us make a cowboy man,
Why not call him long, tall Dan?

First, Dan has a smiling face,
So let's put it right in place.

Then there's a hat for this cowboy man,
Which is his drinking cup and fan.

His shirt, heavy cotton or wool, remember,
Can be worn from June to December.

His red handkerchief protects his face,
When he is riding in a dusty place.

His gloves are worn to protect his hands,
When roping, tying and using brands.

The cowboy's pants are the color blue,
These Levis last the whole year through.

The cowboy's belt may bear his name,
Or the fancy buckle can do the same.

His leather boots are strong and sturdy,
And keep his feet from getting wet and dirty.

The chaps are a pair of leather pants,
That help him when riding by cactus plants.

Now that we've seen the clothes of long, tall Dan,
We know that he's really a cowboy man!

L'IL COWPOKES

DAN

LANGUAGE
continued

Completing Pictures

Recognizing a picture as being complete, is essential to detail in drawing. Use individual drawings from comic strips (simple line drawings) and cut each picture in half. Mounting the whole picture on cardboard and then cutting is best. Hold up half of one picture and line up three other halves (include the matching half). Children should take turns selecting the half that correctly completes the picture.

Completing Pictures

Using an easel, a large sheet of paper and a marking pen, draw a picture the children can complete. Be obvious! Draw a face without eyes and invite someone to complete it for you. Draw a person without legs, a car without tires or a stem without a flower. Allow the children to complete the pictures as creatively as they wish.

FINGER

"Five Little Cowboys"

"Five little cowboys sitting on a gate,
The first one said, 'Gee, rodeos are great!'
The second one said, 'There're buzzards in the air.'
The third one said, 'But we don't care.'
The fourth one said, 'Let's watch the horses run.'
The fifth one said, 'I'm ready for some fun!'
Oooooooo went the wind and off went their hats,
And the five little cowboys fell from where they sat."

Counting to Twelve

Counting up to twelve can be easily practiced using empty egg cartons. Each number is isolated by its own little cup, and therefore encourages the manipulation of each item as it is counted. Cups can be filled with coins, marbles or marshmallows.

Counting Reinforcement

This time, the children will count to twelve and put the items into the cups using sugar tongs. This helps develop the fine motor skills and complicates the counting process.

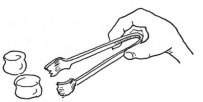

Twelve is a Dozen

Every time there are twelve of the same object, we call it a dozen. What things besides eggs come in a dozen?

SCIENCE LIFE SKILLS

Tools

Explain to the children that tools are simple machines that people use to make work easier. Have pictures available of simple tools, (screw, screwdriver, ax, scissors, nails, wheelbarrow, wheel.) Ask students to explain how each of these items is used. How do they make a job easier? Have students find simple tools in magazines, cut them out and paste them on construction paper. Write the name of the simple tool at the bottom of the paper.

Inclined Plane

Place the end of a ruler on the end of a block, and place a toy truck at the high end of a slope so it will roll down. Now, place the ruler on a higher object and let the toy truck roll down. Ask which truck will roll faster. Ask why. Explain that the "steeper" a slope, the faster a truck will roll down. A board used to make the slope is called an "inclined plane." Put a heavy plank or board on the edge of a chair. Let the other end rest against the wall. Be sure someone holds the chair steady for the child doing the experiment. Have someone step on the board near the wall and walk up to the chair. Ask if it was easy or hard to do. Now take the board away and ask someone to step up onto the chair without help. Was it easier to use the board? Relate how ramps make it easier for handicapped people to get around. Have students explain why.

An inclined plane makes work easier! You will need a heavy object, a low table and a board. Put the heavy object next to the table and challenge each child to see if she can lift the object up on the table. "Who thinks she is strong enough to lift this object up to the table?" Try it! Then show them how easy it can be done by using an inclined plane. Lean the board (board to balance beam) against the table. Begin edging the heavy object up the board to the table. It's easy!

Developing Motor Skills

Pound nails into logs or boards. Saw boards with small saws. Use a plane to make wood curls. All these strengthen coordination and develop motor skills.

Dance

There are many simple square dances the children can learn. Most public libraries have square dance records complete with instructions that can be checked out. If the steps are too complicated for younger children, just teach them a few calls such as "swing your partner," "join hands and circle," and make up your own dances to some country and western music.

Cowboy Songs

Cowboy songs are very simple and easy to learn. Again, your public library is the best resource for these. "Home on the Range," "Red River Valley," "I'm Going To Leave Old Texas Now" are probably familiar enough not to need any music. Don't overlook singing to recordings. Some of the children may have some records to share with the class.

Printing

There are lots of ways to print messages and lots of things that can be used to print with. Below are a number of suggestions for printing activities. Try a new one each day, and then experiment with some you make up yourself!

Branding Iron Scarves

Materials needed: unbleached muslin cut into triangles large enough to go around a child's neck and tie in front like a scarf, brown tempera paint, old branding irons or a tool to use for branding. (Try carving out an old potato, or glue rope onto cardboard in the shape of a brand.)

Have the child dip the brand into the paint and then onto the scarf. Be sure that the paint is no more than ¼ inch deep in the container so that only the raised portion of the brand is coated with paint. Let the scarves dry and then tie them on the children.

Other Types of Printing: Many other objects can be used for printing activities. Here are some suggestons: pieces of sponge held by pinch clothespins; cross sections of various fruits and vegetables (potatoes, oranges, onions and carrots); yarn glued onto cardboard in designs; Styrofoam cut into shapes; household silverware (forks, spatulas or peelers); spools, bobbins and buttons.

Paper: Try printing on different surfaces to experiment with texture. Some suggestions: newspaper, cardboard, wallpaper samples, burlap, wrapping paper, paper plates, cellophane, aluminum foil, sandpaper.

ART
continued

COOK
TO LEARN

Rodeo Bull

Materials needed: brown construction paper; white, black and cream paper; small piece of red for the tongue; glue.

Pre-cut the pieces and help the children assemble the rodeo bull. Discuss how some cowboys like to ride bulls in the rodeo. Crayons may be used to draw the eyes and nostrils.

—————————— **Have a Cookout!** ——————————

Food can be prepared ahead and eaten outside around a pretend campfire. Or, a real campfire can be made to warm up the beans 'n franks and cocoa.

Cowboy Beans and Franks

1 large can ranch-style beans
1 package hot dogs

Cook hot dogs in pan of hot water. Slice into sections. Open can of beans and put into large pot. Add hot dogs and simmer.

Cocoa

1 package chocolate drink mix
milk

Make chocolate drink according to package directions. Heat until hot. Stir while heating.

Biscuits

1 package biscuit mix

Follow directions on box to make biscuits. Can be made a day ahead of time and refrigerated until cookout time. Serve with honey for a cowboy treat!

Cornmeal Pancakes

Beat 2 eggs
Add 2 cups sour milk or buttermilk
Add 4 tablespoons oil

Combine with
1¼ cup flour
1 cup cornmeal
2 teaspoons baking powder
1 teaspoon baking soda
1 teaspoon salt
2 tablespoons sugar

Cook like regular pancakes.

Anglund, Joan Walsh. **The Brave Cowboy.** New York: Harcourt Brace Jovanovich, 1959.
> A small cowboy goes through the day facing bravely the different activities of a real cowboy.

Greene, Carla. **Cowboys—What Do They Do?** New York: Harper & Row, 1972.
> A book that answers the questions about the things cowboys do.

Krasilovsky, Phyllis. **The Girl Who Was a Cowboy.** New York: Doubleday Publishing Co., 1965.
> Although Margaret loves to wear cowboy hats for everyday wear, she finds that flowered hats can also be nice.

Martini, Teri. **The True Book of Cowboys.** Chicago, IL: Childrens Press, 1955.
> The life of a cowboy is explained from the clothes he wears to his different activities and responsibilities on the ranch.

Rounds, Glen. **The Cowboy Trade.** New York: Holiday House, 1972.
> Traces the cowboy's day, his trade, equipment and how he is viewed today.

Shapp, Charles and Martha. **Let's Find Out About Cowboys.** New York: Franklin Watts, 1963.
> A beginning book describing the life of the cowboy.

Color the oldest cowboy's hat yellow.
Color the youngest cowboy's hat blue.
Color the other cowboys' hats any color you like.

Help the stray horse find its way back to the stable.

AMERICAN INDIANS

NOTES

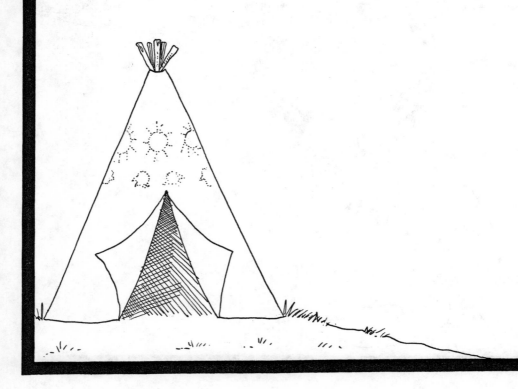

AMERICAN INDIANS

Vocabulary

Indian, native American, tribe, tepee, hogan, pottery, blankets, chief, brave, squaw.

Between

Play a game of "put the penny." Place the penny **between** two objects. Start by putting two objects on a tray (example—pencil and a rock) and placing the penny between the two objects. Say, "The penny is **between** the rock and the pencil." Add another object (block). Now change the position of the penny and say, "The penny is **between** the pencil and the block." Change the position several times, always describing the penny as **between** two of the objects. Now play the game with the children. The children are to "put the penny" as you describe where it should go. Next, have one child "put the penny" and another child describe where it is. The children should now be using the term "between."

Variation: Another day, play the "between" game and use only the objects, eliminating the penny. Increase the number of objects to about five, and cover the tray of objects with a towel each time you rearrange them. This makes the game suspenseful and holds the children's attention. As you uncover the tray, ask which object is **between** two other objects. "What is between the rock and the block?"—the pencil. Again, change the game so that the children use the term **between.**

Listen and Guess

Learning to identify an object from its physical description is an important skill in listening and recognizing characteristics. Put a variety of objects on a tray and give each child a turn at guessing what you will describe. Use only physical characteristics in your descriptions, such as color, size and shape. Alternate roles so that each child describes an object for you to guess.

Sharing

Discuss situations in which you would share things. Why is it necessary? Can it be fun? Now, set up situations and encourage the children to think of ways to share. Bring out an apple. "There are so many of us and only one apple. How can we **share** it?" Do it! Bring out a box of blocks. "There are so many of us and only one box of blocks. How can we **share** them?" Divide them up. Bring a piece of chalk. "There are so many of us and only one piece of chalk. How can we **share** it?" Break it or take turns. Make up more sharing situations. You may want to continue verbally, talking about sharing toys. Allow children to formulate decisions.

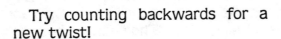
Counting to Ten

Have some fun with math! Play "Ten Little Indians." Let the children improvise a game around this song. They can use their fingers or toes, counting sticks or beads, or they can act out the parts of the Indians. This could also be used for flannel board activities.

Try counting backwards for a new twist!

Patterns

Children get experience in completing a sequence by stringing beads in a **pattern.** Demonstrate by stringing and verbalizing a pattern yourself (cube, cube, sphere; cube, cube, sphere; cube, cube, sphere). It is important that the tone of your voice indicate a pattern also. Be expressive! Now express only a part of the pattern (cube, cube, _____ what comes next?) Encourage the children to make their own bead patterns. Some may wish to make a color pattern instead of a shape pattern.

Pattern Strips

Have available strips of construction paper about three inches wide to create pattern strips with the children. Use buttons, cotton balls or toothpicks. Demonstrate by gluing a pattern to one strip (button, button, cotton ball; button, button, cotton ball). Verbalize the pattern as you create it. Allow the children to make their own pattern strips.

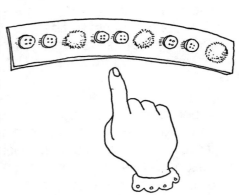

Fossils

Explain to the children that they can learn about plants and animals that lived long ago by studying certain kinds of stones. Some rocks have dents or prints made by animals or plants that lived and died long ago. These dents or prints that are found on rocks are called "fossils." Have examples of fossils for the children to examine. A magnifying glass adds to the enjoyment. Pictures will also suffice if specimens are not available. Give each child a ball of clay or play dough. Have the children press objects onto the clay or play dough to make pretend fossils.

Vibration and Sound

Tell the children that you can **feel** sound. Demonstrate by:
1. Plucking a stretched rubber band.
2. Tapping a drum.
3. Holding your hand to the throat while talking.
4. Plucking a ruler held to the edge of a table.

Do not define **vibration** but use it—"It vibrates!"

SCIENCE
continued

─────────────── **Playing Indian** ───────────────

Children love dressing up and playing "Indian." Make headbands and feathers from construction paper. Poster paints or fluorescent paints can be used to decorate faces. Or, if the teacher prefers, pieces of colored tape can be applied to faces. Some piano music can provide a background for a rain dance.

─────────────── **Manipulating Clay** ───────────────

This is a useful exercise in finger dexterity and creativity. Allow for experimentation. Demonstrate how to make the clay pliable by kneading, pulling and pinching. Have various tools for working the clay available, such as craft sticks, elastic bands, straws or coins. You may want to play a game in which the children hide their eyes while you hide an object under a flattened piece of clay. They guess what the object is by looking at the impression it has made.

Clay Bowls

Demonstrate how clay is used to shape household objects. Perhaps you have some pottery made of clay to show the children. Let them make bowls, spoons or cups out of the clay. Put each finished item on a piece of construction paper with child's name. Arrange the items on a table or bookcase for a pottery show.

Paper Plate Masks

Get some ten-inch paper plates, paint them with tempera and decorate. You can use paper, yarn, sequins, material scraps or anything you want to make your mask colorful. Cut out the eye holes and attach strings or elastic. The teacher can make masks for certain story characters and children can act out parts of the story as the teacher reads it. Many American myths and legends are ideal for this.

ART
continued

SKILLS

TO LEARN

Macaroni Necklaces

Buy macaroni in the grocery store. Be sure the macaroni has a hole through it and is straight (not elbow macaroni). Soak for two to three minutes in water with food coloring, rinse and dry thoroughly. Thread large tapestry needles (blunt ones) with yarn. Thread macaroni on yarn and make a necklace or bracelet.

———————————————— Sewing ————————————————

Help the children learn a basic running stitch by sewing with yarn, a large eye needle and burlap cloth. Stress that the needle goes in one side and out the other; then turn the fabric over and repeat. Children tend to put the needle through the fabric from one side, wrap the thread around the edge of the fabric and go through the same side again. Encourage **turning the fabric over** before the next stitch.

———————————————— Indian Fry Bread ————————————————

1 cup shortening
4 cups flour
1 tablespoon baking powder
1 teaspoon salt
2 tablespoons powdered milk
1½ cups warm water

Mix all ingredients together. Pour in 1½ cups warm water and mix with hands until soft. Pat a small amount back and forth between hands and pull until flat and round. Fry in 1 cup lard (melted) until brown. Sprinkle powdered sugar over warm fry bread or spoon honey over bread.

Cornmeal Cookies

1½ cups shortening
1½ cups sugar
2 eggs
2 teaspoons vanilla
2 cups flour
2 teaspoons baking powder
½ teaspoon salt
2 cups cornmeal

Mix all ingredients in a large bowl. Drop by teaspoon onto greased baking sheet. Bake at 350° for 15 minutes.

Wheat Germ Cornbread

⅔ cup flour
4 teaspoons baking powder
6 tablespoons sugar
1 teaspoon salt
⅔ cup cornmeal
⅓ cup wheat germ
2 eggs, slightly beaten
1 cup milk
4 tablespoons cooking oil

COOK

TO LEARN
continued

Mix all ingredients in a large bowl. Pour into a greased 9 x 9 inch pan and bake at 400° for 30 to 40 minutes.

Johnnycake

1 cup cornmeal
1 cup flour
⅓ cup sugar
5 teaspoons baking powder
1 teaspoon salt

1 cup milk
1 egg
2 tablespoons butter

Mix all ingredients in a large bowl. Add 1 cup milk, 1 beaten egg and 2 tablespoons melted butter. Mix well after each ingredient. Pour into a greased 9 x 9 inch pan. Bake at 425° for 15 minutes.

Chocolate Chip Pumpkin Bread

4 eggs
2½ cups sugar
1 cup oil
⅓ cup water
2 cups canned pumpkin
3½ cups flour
2 teaspoons soda
1½ teaspoons salt
1 teaspoon cinnamon
chocolate chips

Beat eggs and sugar together. Add oil, water and pumpkin to egg mixture. Mix flour, soda, salt and cinnamon together and add to pumpkin mixture. Stir in as many chocolate chips as you like (usually between 6 to 12 ounces). Pour into 2 or 3 greased bread pans. Bake at 300° for 1½ hours.

Clark, Ann Nolan. **The Little Indian Basket Maker.** Chicago, IL: Melmont Publishers, 1957.
> A Papago Indian girl learns about basket making from her grandmother by helping gather and prepare yucca leaves and weaving a mat from them.

Clark, Ann Nolan. **The Little Indian Pottery Maker.** Chicago, IL: Melmont Publishers, 1955.
> A little Pueblo Indian girl tells how she learns from her mother to work with clay while doing woman's work.

Hoff, Syd. **Little Chief.** New York: Harper & Row, 1961.
> Little Chief discovers new friends from a passing wagon train who teach him new games. He, in turn, teaches them things that he has been taught to do.

Parish, Peggy. **Little Indian.** New York: Simon & Schuster, 1968.
> Little Indian wants his very own special name, searches the woods and returns to the village with a name that surprises him.

Russel, Solveig Paulson. **Navaho Land.** Chicago, IL: Melmont Publishers, 1961.
> This book discusses life on the Navaho reservation, including such topics as food, clothing, shelter, sheep raising, jewelry making and religious ceremonies.

Shapp, Charles. **Let's Find Out About Indians.** New York: Franklin Watts, 1962.
> This book tells "how Indians got their food and clothing, about the different kinds of homes the Indians lived in and the games which Indian boys and girls played."

Draw dot to dot to find a hunting tool used by early American Indians.

.1

.2

.3

.4

.5

6

FRIENDS
AROUND
THE WORLD

NOTES

FRIENDS AROUND THE WORLD

Vocabulary

Piñata, fiesta, hula, sphere, cube, cylinder, pyramid, cone, magnify, gracias, por favor, buenos días, adiós, merci, bonjour, s'il vous plâit, adieu, danke, hallo, bitte sehr, auf Wiedersehen, arigato, ohayo, tanoshimaseru, sayonara.

Homes

Have travel brochures from different lands showing pictures of the homes found there. You can find other pictures of homes in social studies books. Have the children look and identify the differences in the homes—roofs, windows, walls and doors. Use the observations as the basis for a discussion about why the roofs are flat in the Greek Islands and pointed in Switzerland, and why the walls are thick in the homes in Mexico and thin in Hawaii.

Courtesy

To help the children become more aware of the importance of courtesy in everyday life and to reinforce basic vocabulary in other languages, have the children respond with the correct answer to these questions:
1. What would you say to a friend who has given you a toy?
2. What would you say to someone who just walked into the room?
3. What would you say if you wanted to borrow an ink pen?
4. What would you say when you leave to go home?

Ask the children, how would you answer these questions in:

French (merci, bonjour, s'il vous plâit, adieu)
Spanish (gracias, buenos días, por favor, adiós)
German (danke, hallo, bitte sehr, auf Wiedersehen)
Japanese (arigato, ohayo, tanoshimaseru, sayonara)

Learning Names

On 3 x 5 inch cards, print children's names with a felt tip pen. Have the children sit in a semicircle on the floor. Hand each child a card with her name on it. Have each child stand and say her name holding out the card. Collect the cards and show each individually to the class. Let the children sound out the letters until they can guess the names. They may already know many of the names from having seen them on the children's lockers. Have the children exchange cards and then take turns saying the name that is written on the card.

FINGER

PLAY MATH

"1-2-3"

"1-2-3 (suit actions to words)
Upon my head my hands, I place,
On my shoulders, on my face,
On my hips, at my side,
Now behind me they will hide.
Now I'll stretch them way up high,
Make my fingers swiftly fly.
I'll hold them up in front of me
and quickly clap 1-2-3."

Measuring Again

Measuring cups, an individual 8-ounce pyrex cup and one-quart or pint pyrex measuring cups with marks make excellent measuring devices. Using sand or rice, ask each child to measure a specific amount. Explain fraction marks on the sides of the measuring cups. Have a set of individual measuring cups and demonstrate how the ½ measuring cup fills the large measuring cup up to the ½ mark. Let the children experiment measuring rice or sand and pouring the measured ingredient into a large bowl or plastic tub.

Recognizing Solid Shapes

Play a game in which the children recognize and name solid shapes (sphere, cube, cylinder, pyramid, cone). Use five containers which will fully cover each solid shape. Place one shape under each cup while saying its name. Ask, "Which cup is hiding the sphere?" If a child uncovers a cube, say, "That is a cube!" and continue with the game. After the children have become familiar with the shapes, ask them to point to a container and guess which shape is under it. In this way, they will be naming as well as recognizing the different shapes.

Expanding Solid Shapes Knowledge

Draw a shaded picture of each solid shape on a piece of construction paper. Place a picture in front of the children. Put the solid shapes into a bucket and allow each child to draw out one shape at a time. The child then matches the shape to the picture of the shape. Encourage the naming of the shapes—sphere, cylinder, cube, pyramid, cone. Matching a real object to a picture of the same object is basic to understanding shapes.

Magnifying

Magnify means to make things look bigger. This explanation is sufficient at the preschool level, but may be elaborated on if questions are asked. Have small paper plates and a variety of things to look at available (coffee, sugar, candy, small objects, letters, numerals). Make sure that you have a small magnifying glass for each child so that everyone can observe at the same time. Use the term **magnify** while talking to the children. Continue this activity by walking around the room and observing items together through a magnifying glass.

Magnifying Reinforcement

Children enjoy using materials that are not often available to them. Set out ink pads and rubber stamps. Let the children experiment. Use magnifying glasses to observe stamped images. Ask the children, "Did you know you have lines on the tips of your fingers? Try to find them with the magnifying glass." Point out that these lines can be seen easier if we make fingerprints. Give each child an index card with her name on it. Let the children ink and print each of their fingers on the card. Encourage them to magnify their fingerprints. Point out that everyone has her own individual fingerprints.

Marches in Music

Marches are a lot of fun. Organize your march as a rhythm band with instruments or just as a march of people. Explain to the children how marches have a specific beat which helps the marchers keep time with the music. Marches can be fast ("Stars and Stripes Forever") or slow ("Wedding March"). Grab your baton, step lively!! Join the parade around the room and outside around the playground.

Maracas

Orange juice cans, empty chip cans or empty soup cans with a handful of beans placed inside make excellent maracas. Put on a Spanish record and dance away!

Mexican Dance

Records can be obtained from your neighborhood library or purchased inexpensively. They come with directions of simple Mexican folk dances. The "Mexican Hat Dance" is an easy one to learn and everyone can do it.

continued

Hula

Another activity involving motor skills and music is the hula. Records are available with music and instructions for simple hulas. Perhaps a mother or a dance instructor would volunteer an hour of her time to come and teach the children. Make crepe paper leis and put on a little show.

Move to Music

There are many ways to move to music. You can lead the children in a hop, jump, crawl, gallop, run, roll or skip activity. Tell the children to use all the muscles in their bodies. Express the music through motion.

──────── Hawaiian Lei ────────

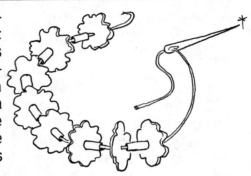

A lei can be made easily from construction paper and drinking straws. Cut flower shapes approximately 1½ inches in diameter from different colored construction paper. Cut straws into 1-inch lengths. Thread a darning needle with a length of yarn and string alternately the flowers and the straw pieces until the right length is achieved. Tie the ends together and wear as a necklace.

Mexican Piñata

Stuff a large paper grocery sack with newspaper. Tie the top of the bag with a piece of twine and mold the bag into a large ball shape. Paint the sack a solid color. Decorate the outside of the piñata with tissue paper that has been cut in 1-inch squares. Fringe can be cut from different colored tissue paper and glued onto the surface in overlapping layers. After the piñata is completed, the newspaper can be removed and the goodies (toys, candies, fruit, money) placed inside. Tie a string to the top of the piñata for hanging.

Variation: Make individual piñatas by using lunch-sized paper bags and the same procedure as above.

Chinese Fans

Fold a 12 x 12 inch square of posterboard in half and cut out two geometric shapes. Glue the two pieces of posterboard together with a tongue depressor placed between the two shapes. Paint the fan and handle with poster paint. When dry, use a felt tip pen to create new and interesting designs on both sides of the fan. Cover with clear contact paper to protect your design and to give your fan reinforcement.

Igloo

Glue circle Styrofoam packing pieces onto an overturned margarine tub or cottage cheese container. Use a felt tip pen to outline the door opening.

Mexican Village

Collect empty boxes of various shapes (toothpaste, perfume, cologne, instant soup). Use pastel tempera paint and paint each box a different color. On a large board or tabletop, press yellow play dough down the center of the table. Have students get small pebbles from the playground and press into the play dough to represent a cobblestone street. Place colored boxes on either side of the street to represent houses. To represent flower pots, separate egg cartons into individual cups and paint them with different pastel tempera paint. Place chunks of play dough into the cup and stick a 4-inch length pipe cleaner into the center. Cut different colored tissue paper into 1-inch squares. Place two or three different colored pieces of tissue paper onto pipe cleaners. Place these throughout the village. Cacti can also be cut out and placed throughout the village.

continued

Japanese Paper Lanterns

Have lots of different colored construction paper (12 x 18 inch) available. Cut a 1-inch strip off the end of the constrction paper to form a lantern handle. Fold the paper in half lengthwise. Draw a line two inches from the open end of the paper. Mark cutting lines from the fold to the heavy line one inch apart. (This can be done by the teacher for very young children.) Cut slits on cutting lines. Unfold the paper and form a cylinder. Staple the ends together. Staple the handle to the top of the lantern. To simulate light, place a piece of crushed red or yellow tissue paper inside the lamp.

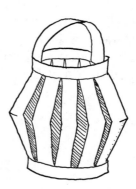

C
O
O
K

TO LEARN

———————————— **Cheese Crisp** ————————————

Place a large flour tortilla with 1 tablespoon of oil on a warm griddle or skillet. Let brown. Turn with spatula and sprinkle with grated cheese. After the cheese melts, remove from pan. Microwave: 30 seconds on high, or until cheese melts.

Tostados

box of round corn chips
1 can (16 oz.) refried beans
½ pound of longhorn cheese

Spread beans on top of corn chips. Grate cheese and sprinkle on top of bean mixture. Place in a 350° oven for 5 minutes or until cheese melts.

Fruit Salad

papaya
pineapple
bananas
strawberries
oranges

Let the children peel, cut and slice the different fruits. Mix in a large bowl and let stand for an hour so the juices blend together. Put servings into individual paper cups. Talk about where the different fruits come from with the children while they are eating the salad.

Wedding Cakes (Bride's Cookies)

½ cup flour
⅛ teaspoon salt
¼ cup butter or margaine
1 tablespoon sugar
½ teaspoon vanilla
½ cup finely ground pecans or walnuts
powdered sugar

Cream butter and sugar. Add flour, salt, vanilla and ground nuts. Mix well. Form into small balls and place on a lightly greased cookie sheet. Bake in a 400° oven for about 10 minutes until lightly browned. Remove from oven and cool slightly for about 3 minutes. Roll immediately in powdered sugar. Repeat when room temperature.

Bim, Lorraine. **Burro That Had a Name.** New York: Harcourt Brace Jovanovich, 1939.
> Chucho decides to call a burro Nacas, meaning "long ears" and because of the name, the runaway burro is found.

Lamorisse, Albert. **The Red Balloon.** New York: Doubleday Publishing Co., 1956.
> A red balloon becomes Pascal's best friend and stays with him until a group of boys attack the balloon with slingshots. Then, something unusual happens.

Matsuno, Masako. **A Pair of Red Clogs.** Cincinnati, OH: World, 1960.
> Mako's new red clogs get cracked playing a game and she is tempted to do a dishonest thing to replace them.

Politi, Leo. **Lito and the Clown.** New York: Scribner, 1964.
> In the middle of a carnival, a Mexican boy searches for his lost kitten and gets help from a stilt-walking clown.

Politi, Leo. **Little Leo.** New York: Scribner, 1951.
> Little Leo decides to take his Indian Chief suit to an Italian village and causes quite a stir.

Politi, Leo. **Piccolo's Prank.** New York: Scribner, 1965.
> Piccolo, an organ grinder's little monkey, jumps from a trolley car and hides underneath until the police and firemen can rescue him.

Politi, Leo. **Rosa.** New York: Scribner, 1963.
> Rosa, a little Mexican girl, yearns for a baby doll in the toy shop window until Christmas brings her a surprise—a new baby sister.

Seignobosc, Francoise. **Jeanne-Marie in Gay Paris.** New York: Scribner, 1956.
> Jeanne-Marie leaves her two friends on the farm and visits her aunt in Paris. She has a wonderful time while searching for a present to bring back to her friends.

Viorst, Judith. **Alexander and the Terrible, Horrible, No Good, Very Bad Day.** New York: Antheneum, 1972.
> Alexander wakes up one day, nothing goes right and he wishes he could go to Australia.

Yashima, Taro. **Crow Boy.** New York: The Viking Press, 1955.
> A shy Japanese boy finds friends through a teacher who understands him.

In each row, one of the instruments is different from the others.
Color the one that is different.

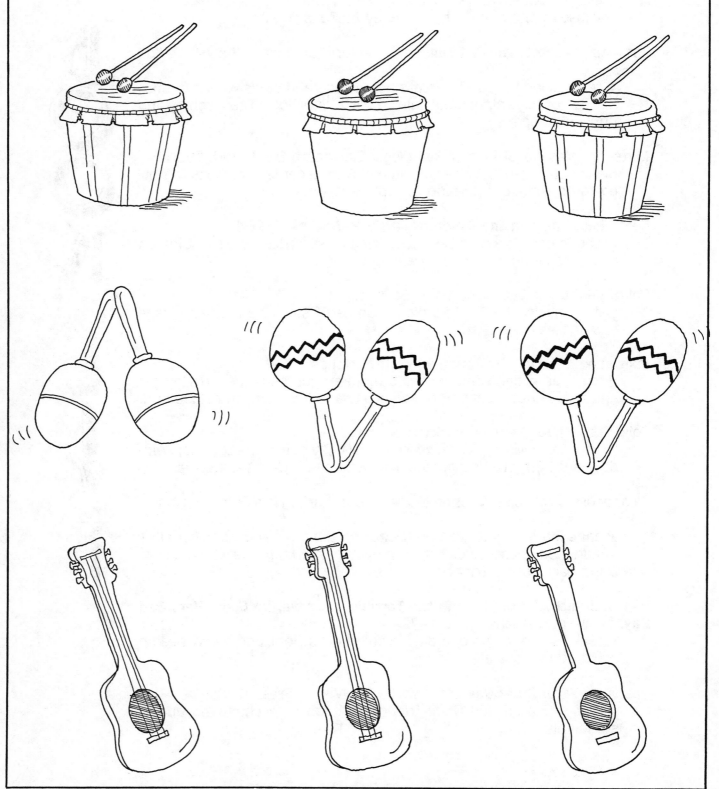

Color the puzzle.
Cut it apart and give it to a friend to put back together again.

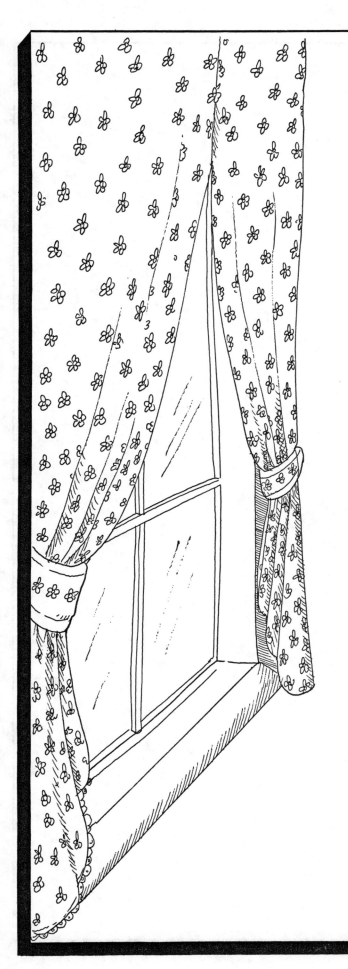

PLANTS

NOTES

PLANTS

Vocabulary

Plants, leaves, flowers, roots, seeds, evergreens, indoor, outdoor, greenhouse, skin, husk, hull, pod, rind, shell, peel.

Alphabet Song

The alphabet song is a means of learning the order of the letters (important for cataloging and alphabetizing). At this stage, children are learning the "words" to a familiar tune. If you listen to many children sing the "LMNOP" segment of the alphabet, it is obvious that they have not "learned" the alphabet but are mimicking the verbal sounds of a song. It is important to identify individual letters within the alphabet sequences.

Sing the words to the alphabet song while pointing to each letter on the board (use chalkboard, bulletin board, magnetic letter board or felt board). Sing slowly enough to touch the letters—one verbal letter for one visual letter. Then, play a game in which the children close their eyes while you remove a letter. "What's missing?" The children guess, and in order to test their predictions again, sing the alphabet song slowly while you point. When you come to the empty space, point and sing the letter that's missing. Allow the children to remove the letters.

"Can Do" Box

Use a card file to make a "can do" box. Make sure the letters on the filing cards are clearly visible. As you say each child's name, print the first letter of his name on a piece of paper. Let him find this same letter in the card file. When he has found the letter, take out a card, print his name on it and encourage him to tell you something he can do. Print exactly what he says on the card. Children enjoy seeing their own words in print. They also gain confidence in their capabilities if encouraged to reflect on their positive points. The box should be made available so that children may enter a "can do" whenever they wish. You may want to begin the activity by finding your own letter and entering a "can do." You'll be demonstrating the idea for the children as well as building your own confidence! The children will enjoy the teacher's "can do" as well.

Seed Protection

Nature protects seeds in very interesting and unusual ways. Bring in examples of seeds and the ways in which they are protected:

skin—cherry, apple
husk—corn
pod—peas
rind—orange, grapefruit
peel—banana
shell—nut
hull—wheat

FINGER PLAY

———————————————— **"Bee Hives"** ————————————————

"Here is the bee hive, where are the bees?
Hidden away where nobody sees. (make fist)
Watch and you'll see them come out of the hive,
1-2-3-4-5. Buzz-z-z-z." (wiggle fingers)

———————————— **Drawing Numerals** ————————————

Children must learn to draw numerals in the same way they draw letters. Make a set of numerals out of sandpaper. Paste the numerals on a sheet of plain construction paper. Make the numerals at least three inches high. Let the child use his index finger to trace the numeral. Fill a pie pan with dry sand about ½-inch deep. After the child has traced the sandpaper numeral, have him "draw the numeral in the dry sand." Be sure to keep repeating the number over and over as the child draws it.

Drawing Large Numerals

Draw the numerals again, this time on large sheets of butcher paper with crayons or wide felt tip pens. Let the children practice writing numerals, making them with large strokes.

———————————————————— **Plants** ————————————————————

Plants are a wonderful way to introduce science to children. Here are some classroom activities involving plants.
• Cut out pictures of food that plants provide for man. Put them on a chart.
• Visit a grocery store and notice the food that is provided by plants.
• Look at what the child is wearing to see if anything he has on comes from plants.
• After a visit to a farm, discuss the ways a farmer uses plants.

Plant Parts

Cut out the parts of a plant from flannel. Have the words: flower, stem, leaves, petals and roots printed on pieces of flannel. Explain to the children that the roots of plants grow downward. The stem grows upward. The leaves and flowers grow from the stem. As the plant grows, it turns toward the sunlight. Have the children take turns placing the plant parts with the correct labels on the flannel board.

Reinforcement: Put parts of the plants on the flannel board. Have the children tell what part of the plant is missing.

Leaves

Bring an assortment of leaves to class. Pass them around for the children to feel.

Do all the leaves feel the same? What words tell us how they feel? What are the different textures and how can you describe them?

Make a leaf collection by gathering an assortment of leaves from the neighborhood and school. Leaves can be saved by placing them between two sheets of waxed paper and pressing them with a medium-hot iron. Display the leaf collection on a bulletin board, hang the pressed leaves from windows or paste them on paper to share with the children's families.

Dish Garden

Plant a dish garden with the children. You don't need soil to make things grow. Fill a shallow dish with water. Have the children help you cut off the tops of a turnip, rutabaga, carrot, pineapple and beet. Also, cut a potato in half. Place each plant in the shallow dish, cut side down. After a few days the greens will grow. These can eventually be transplanted to soil and new plants started. You may want to put food coloring in the water to observe the vein system each plant has.

Grow Your Own

Go to a health food store and buy a bag of alfalfa seeds. Soak them overnight and put them into a wire strainer over a bowl. Twice daily, rinse them with clean water. When the sprouts are long enough, sprinkle them on egg salad or tuna salad snacks.

continued

Stir-Fry Bean Sprouts

Bean sprouts are easy to grow. Use the same method as that used for alfalfa sprouts. When the bean sprouts are ready, prepare them in the following manner: fry a few strips of bacon until crisp; drain and crumble. Put bean sprouts in hot bacon fat. Toss for a few seconds until just heated but not cooked. Remove from pan. Stir in bacon bits and serve.

Watch 'em Grow

To actually see seeds grow, place lima beans in small paper cups along with wet cotton balls. Place the cups next to a light source. Keep the cotton balls wet, and in a few days you will see the young plants emerge from the seed.

• Plant some different seeds (corn, grass or radishes) using the same procedure as the lima beans. Watch the germination of these seeds.

• As the seeds continue germinating, watch the seed coat shrivel and eventually fall off. Then, watch the roots and finally the stem start to develop.

• Continue experimenting with the seeds by planting some of the germinating seeds in soil and leaving the others in the water solution in the paper cups. Keep a record of which ones continue to do well and which ones do not.

• Point out to the children that as the seed coats shrivel and die, the true food-making leaves develop and the seeds now get their nourishment from the nutrients in the soil.

Other Seed Activities

Point out to the children that not all seeds are planted by people. Seeds move in some unusual ways. The wind can carry them to a new place. They can stick to the fur of animals and then drop off in a different place, and animals such as squirrels and mice can carry them to another place.

• A plant will naturally turn toward the light. Place several plants on a window ledge and watch them bend toward the sunlight. Every day turn one plant around. Leave the other plants alone. Note the difference in the way the plants are growing.

• Put one of your plants in a cupboard or closet. After three days, take it out and compare it to the ones on the windowsill. Is there a difference? Do plants need light? What color are the leaves?

Growing Make Believe

Rain makes the flowers and plants grow. Let's see what rain and sun can do for a seed. Have the children lie on the floor curled up in a ball to represent a seed. Pretend it is rainy, then sunny. Slowly the seed begins to grow and uncurl and push up through the soil. Children can slowly begin to stand and extend arms to represent leaves and branches. Children may enjoy improvising piano music to give background to the rainy part and to the sunny part.

Plant Collage

Toddlers love to go on walks to gather leaves and small seeds, and to have the opportunity to glue these treasures on paper. Always remember—any one little item on paper can be a major accomplishment! Squeeze-on glue works well.

Vegetable Printmaking

Cut oranges, cucumbers, apples, onions and lettuce in cross sections. Dip the sections into thick tempera paint and make prints on construction paper. The texture of the vegetable creates an interesting effect.

Leaf Rubbings

Take a walking field trip to collect leaves. When you return to the room, make leaf rubbings. Place the leaves under paper. Show the children how to use the side of a crayon to make a "magic picture." If the shape tends to move, it can be glued to cardboard then placed under the children's papers.

Chunky Peanut Butter Spread

1 4-ounce package whipped cream cheese
½ cup chunky peanut butter
2 tablespoons milk
1 tablespoon honey
½ cup finely snipped raisins or dried apricots
flaked coconut (optional)
apple or pear slices
crackers

Steps for making spread:
1. Collect all ingredients.
2. In a small mixing bowl, stir together the cream cheese and peanut butter.
3. Add milk, 1 tablespoon at a time, stirring until blended. Stir in honey.
4. Stir in raisins or apricots. Using a rubber spatula, scrape mixture into a serving bowl.
5. Sprinkle coconut on top if desired. Arrange fruit slices and crackers on a serving plate with spread. Refrigerate any leftovers in a covered container. Makes 1½ cups.

DRAMA

ART

COOK
TO LEARN

Raw Fruit and Vegetables

For the child, this activity involves peeling, cutting and taking out the seeds. Fruits and vegetables can be tasted raw, and some can later be boiled or stewed. This activity can lead to a lot of related discussions about how different foods look when raw and when cooked, and how they feel and taste.

TO LEARN
continued

Peanut Butter

1½ cups salted peanuts
1 tablespoon oil

(shelling peanuts is an excellent motor development activity. Save the shells for a collage activity.)

Place peanuts in blender with lid on. Turn to high speed. Blend until smooth. Add 1 tablespoon oil and blend until mixed.

Gorp

1 cup dry roasted peanuts
1 cup raisins
1 cup sunflower seeds
1 cup M&M's
1 cup coconut (optional)

Combine all ingredients and pour mixture into a jar. Cover and keep the jar out of the sun so the M&M's won't melt.

Bulla, Clyde Robert. **A Tree Is a Plant.** New York: Thomas Y. Crowell, 1960.
> Using a simple text, the author takes the young reader through the life cycle of the apple tree, from seed through flowering to fruit.

Hurd, Edith Thacher. **This Is the Forest.** New York: Coward-McCann, 1969.
> Describes the gradual but constant process of new growth. A good beginning ecology book.

Lerner, Sharon. **I Found A Leaf.** Minneapolis, MN: Lerner Publications, 1964.
> This book explains various leaves and the trees they come from.

Podendorf, Illa. **The True Book of Trees.** Chicago, IL: Childrens Press, 1954.
> This book introduces the parts of a tree and their functions, as well as the kinds of trees and their place in the environment.

Podendorf, Illa. **The True Book of Weeds and Flowers.** Chicago, IL: Childrens Press, 1955.
> This book identifies the various types of weeds and why they are harmful, and shows the beauty of wildflowers.

Selsam, Millicent E., and Hunt, Joyce. **A First Look At the World of Plants.** New York: Walker and Co., 1978.
> An introduction to the plant life that surrounds us.

Shecter, Ben. **Partouche Plants a Seed.** New York: Harper & Row, 1966.
> Partouche, a pig, and his friend Raymond, a field mouse, find a seed, plant it and care for the new plant.

Udry, Janice May. **A Tree Is Nice.** New York: Harper & Row, 1956.
> A beautiful picture book showing the many delights to be found around a tree, such as picking apples, swinging or raking leaves.

Zion, Gene. **Plant Sitter.** New York: Harper & Row, 1959.
> Tommy earns money taking care of the plants of the neighbors who go on vacation, but the plants get out of control, making Tommy and his family uncomfortable.

Plants need sunlight, water and air to grow.
Draw some healthy plants in this garden.

Here is a plant for you to color.
Color the leaves green.
Color the stem brown.
Color the flower red.

NOTES

ZOO SAFARI

Vocabulary

Safari, zoo, lion, tiger, giraffe, elephant, alligator, rhinoceros, hippopotamus, ostrich, kangaroo, buffalo, deer, antelope, paw, hoof, beak, claw, horn, wing, fin, antenna, mane.

Naming Animals

Have the children sit in a circle on the floor. You may begin by saying, "I went to the zoo and I saw a _____." Insert the name of an animal that might be found at the zoo. The next child continues by repeating the sentence and inserting the name of a different animal that would be found at the zoo. Each child takes a turn and tries to name an animal that has not been named before.

Packing for a Safari I

The children will need old magazines and catalogs for this activity. Explain to the children what a safari is. Point out that when one goes on safari, it is necessary to take all sorts of things, such as tents, sleeping bags and food. Let the children cut pictures from magazines of things they would like to take on safari. Glue the pictures to white paper and beneath each object write its name. Tack the pictures on a bulletin board titled "Packing for a Safari."

Packing for a Safari II

The next day, have the children sit in a half circle around the bulletin board. Call each child's name and have the child come up, point to the picture she cut out and tell why that object was selected.

Parts of Animals

You will need pictures of zoo animals for this activity. Hold up a picture of a lion and ask, "Does a lion have wings?" The children should respond, "No." Then ask, "What does a lion have?" The children can then name all the parts of a lion, such as its ears, claws, tail and mane. Additional questions may be asked such as, "Where do we find lions?" "What do lions eat?" "What are lion babies called?" "How do lions move?" Work with only three or four animals each day.

Breaking a Sequence

The skill of classiying objects must be used to complete this task. Choose four of the nested blocks, making sure there is a noticeable difference in size. Sequence them in order from the smallest to the largest. Ask the children to close their eyes while you remove one block and push the rest together to fill in the space. Then ask a child to replace the block in sequence. Continue until every child has had a turn. At the end of the lesson, mix up all the blocks and give each child a chance to arrange them in proper sequence.

Breaking a Sequence Follow-up

Play a game of rearranging the blocks using the entire set of nesting blocks. This allows for finer size discrimination. This time you should remove two blocks from the sequence.

Empty Sets

Play a game in which a set having nothing in it is called an "empty" set. Have teddy bear counters or other small plastic animals available. Use paper cups to represent their cages at the zoo. Fill all the cups with an animal except one. Explain that this cage is empty and represents an empty set. Children might want to make up reasons why the cage is empty: they are cleaning it, the animals have gone to the vet, the cage is broken.

Empty Set Follow-up

The next day, play a word game about empty sets. Ask the children silly questions for which the answers will be "an empty set." For instance, "How many purple toads are sitting on the piano?" "How many chocolate doughnuts are hanging from the light fixture?"

Baby Elephant Pantomime

Obtain the recording of "Baby Elephant Walk" or "The Pink Panther" from your local library. For "Baby Elephant Walk," the children can pretend that they are baby elephants by clasping their hands, bending over and swinging their arms like a trunk. For "Pink Panther," the children can pretend to be partners in the jungle walking and stalking smoothly and quietly. They can look from right to left for something to pounce on and eat!

Wild Animals Pantomime

Little children love acting out favorite stories. A good activity for the Safari unit is acting out some of the JUST SO STORIES by Rudyard Kipling. These can be found in any library. Three good ones to use are, "How the Rhinocerous Got Its Skin," "How the Elephant Got Its Trunk," and "How the Camel Got Its Hump." Read the story to the children. Discuss the awkward walk of a camel or the snap of a crocodile's jaws. Select a few children to act out the story as you reread it for the children. A different story can be selected for each day.

Paper Lions

They're easy! All you need is yellow, gold or tan construction paper, yarn, felt tip pens, scissors and paste. Take a piece of 4 x 7 inch paper and cut a semicircle out of the center. Turn the semicircle upside down and paste on the upper left-hand corner of paper. Surround the lion's face with yarn fringe and add a fringe tail. Draw on eyes, nose and whiskers.

A Mask for Leo

Paint a small paper plate either light brown or gold. Next, cut out a hole for the mouth and two holes for eyes. Cut several 2-inch pieces of yarn and glue around the edge of the plate to make the lion's mane. Use black or brown yarn and glue on whiskers and other features. Poke a hole in each side of the mask and insert a yarn tie.

Clothespin Alligator

Take two wooden clothespins and clamp them together with the open ends facing each other. Secure with glue. Clamp another clothespin to the top stick of the clothespin on the left and glue in place. This makes the clothespin on the right the alligator's head, the one in the middle, the body and the one on the left, the tail. Paint the alligator green. When the green paint has dried, paint the inside of the mouth red and glue in a slender strip of red felt for the tongue. Glue eyes to each side of the head.

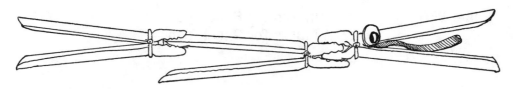

ART
continued

Paper Bag Elephant

Start with a medium-sized grocery bag. Stuff the bottom half with crumpled newspaper and tie that section off with string. Twist the unstuffed front of the bag tightly to form a trunk. Tie the end. Cut two half circles for ears and glue on either side. Pinch on four wooden clothespins for legs. Add paper eyes and a bit of yarn for a tail. He's all ready to stand on your zoo shelf.

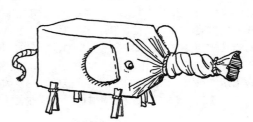

SKILLS

———————— **Dust** ————————

Dust is everywhere! It makes people sneeze! It floats in the air and settles on everything. Look at the dust in a shaft of sunlight. The particles are so small that you usually cannot see them. Where else do you find dust? On the playground? On furniture? On the bottom of your shoe? How can you make dust? By slapping together two erasers? That makes eraser dust. What do we do to get rid of dust so we don't sneeze? Give the children dust cloths and let them dust the furniture and fixtures in the room. Compare the dust on each other's cloths. Who would have thought the room had so much dust in it?!

———————— **Zebra Brownies** ————————

1 package brownie mix
1 package (3 oz.) cream cheese
3 tablespoons butter or margarine
¼ cup sugar
3 eggs
1 tablespoon flour
½ teaspoon vanilla

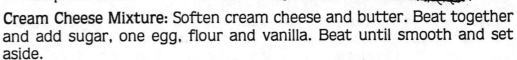

Cream Cheese Mixture: Soften cream cheese and butter. Beat together and add sugar, one egg, flour and vanilla. Beat until smooth and set aside.

Brownie Batter: Empty brownie mix into medium-sized bowl. Add 2 tablespoons water and 2 eggs. Mix by hand 50 strokes. Pour half the brownie batter into greased 8 x 8 or 9 x 9 inch square pan. Spread cream cheese mixture over brownie layer. Spoon remaining brownie batter in dollops over cream cheese batter. Pull knife through batter in swirls.

Bake: 350° for 35-40 minutes for 8 inch pan
            30-35 minutes for 9 inch pan

TO LEARN

Guifoile, Elizabeth. **Nobody Listens to Andrew.** Chicago, IL: Follett, 1957.
Andrew discovers something upstairs and tries to tell his family and his neighbor, but no one will listen.

Leyendrost, Robert. **The Snake That Sneezed.** New York: Putnam, 1970.
While seeking his fortune, Harold meets and then swallows many different animals. After a gigantic snake sneeze, the animals find themselves in new situations.

Mayer, Mercer. **What Do You Do with a Kangaroo?** New York: Four Winds, 1974.
A little girl can find no solution to her unique problem. Many different animals want to sleep in her bed, eat her cereal, drink her bath water and wear her clothes.

Sivulich, Sandra Stoner. **I'm Going on a Bear Hunt.** New York: Dutton, 1973.
A boy encounters many obstacles in his search for a bear.

Skorpen, Liesel Moak. **If I Had a Lion.** New York: Harper & Row, 1967.
A little girl imagines how much fun she would have with a lion for a pet.

Snyder, Dick. **One Day at the Zoo.** New York: Scribner, 1960.
A collection of exciting photographs of the animals of the San Diego Zoo.

Waber, Bernard. **An Anteater Named Arthur.** Boston, MA: Houghton Mifflin, 1967.
Arthur questions why he is called an anteater and why his mother is upset with his room, but his brother provides him with the answers.

Waber, Bernard. **Lyle, Lyle, Crocodile.** Boston, MA: Houghton Mifflin, 1965.
Mr. Grump and his cat, Loretta, are upset about Lyle living with the Primm family, but Lyle proves his friendship in an heroic gesture.

Ward, Lyn. **The Biggest Bear.** Boston, MA: Houghton Mifflin, 1952.
In looking for the biggest bear, Johnny finds a small cub which he brings home to raise. He encounters many problems as the bear grows rapidly and becomes quite large.

Wildsmith, Brian. **Wild Animal.** New York: Watts, 1967.
A beautiful picture book explaining what different groups of wild animals are called.

Draw a line from each animal to the body part belonging to it.

Color the animal that works with its trunk.
Draw a stripe for the baby skunk.
Now, give the giraffe another spot or two,
And you will have your very own zoo!

NOTES

THE FARM

Vocabulary

Farmer, dairy, tractor, hay, barn, silo, horse, cow, pig, chicken, goat.

Flannel Board—"The Little Chick"

Pre-cut shapes from yellow, orange and black felt. Use pinking shears for the yellow circles to add texture and variety. Follow the steps to create the chick on the flannel board. Then let the children come to the flannel board one at a time and put the chick together as you read the steps.

"A new baby came to the farm today.
He looks like a powder puff, they say.

His little yellow head is a fluffy ball.
He doesn't have much tail at all.

A triangle of orange is his little beak.
It helps him eat and lets him speak.

Two little eyes help him find his Mom,
And see all the animals on the farm.

His skinny legs he uses to run,
When playing with other chicks in the sun.

With three little toes he scratches the ground,
To look for worms that must be found.

He plays with his brothers and sisters in the barn,
And at night they all snuggle with Mom to keep warm."

"Eensy Weensy Spider"

"The eensy, weensy spider
Climbed up the water spout.
(alternate index finger and thumb in climbing motion)

Down came the rain and
Washed the spider out!
(hands with fingers wiggling come down and then move to side)

Out came the sun and
dried up all the rain.
(arms form circle above head)

And the eensy weensy spider
Climbed up the spout again."
(repeat first climbing motion)

FINGER PLAY
continued

"Sleepy"

"Sleepy, sleepy the cow went to bed for the night.	(hands, palms together, held beside head)
Sleepy, sleepy the cow went to bed for the night.	(repeat above action)
Moo, moo, the cow woke up in the morning."	(hands on each side of head, open with palms forward, framing face)

Repeat substituting different farm animals and their sounds.

"The Little Green Frog"

"Um! Ah! Went the little green frog one day.	(on Um!—close eyes tight and scrunch up face)
Um! Ah! went the little green frog. Um! Ah! Went the little green frog one day. Um! Ah! Um!"	(on Ah!—open eyes wide and open mouth with tongue sticking out)

--- **Create Animal Shapes** ---

You can cut out a large number of basic shapes from colored construction paper, and the children can use these to create animal shapes. You may have to demonstrate by showing how a circle can be a face and two triangles, the ears. Smaller circles can be eyes and a rectangle can be used for a body. First, arrange the shapes on a piece of white construction paper and then glue them in place. The children can make real-life animals found on the farm or they can make strange, imaginary animals for a farm on Mars. They can even make up crazy names for their Martian animals.

--- **"The Farmer in the Dell"** ---

"The farmer in the dell,
The farmer in the dell,
Hi-Ho the dairy-o
The farmer in the dell.

The farmer takes a wife, etc.
The wife takes a child, etc.
The child takes the nurse, etc.
The nurse takes the dog, etc.
The dog takes the cat, etc.
The cat takes the rat, etc.
The rat takes the cheese, etc.
The cheese stands alone, etc."

Animals and Babies

Cut out pictures of pets or farm animals and their babies from magazines and old picture books, and paste the pictures on oak tag or stiff paper. Tell the children that baby animals are not always called by the same names as their mothers. Examples can include cat—kitten, dog—puppy, sheep—lamb, pig—piglet, cow—calf, deer—fawn, swan—cygnet, duck—duckling, goose—gosling, fox—kit. Give the name of the animals and have the children match the correct baby animal name. Use farm and domesticated animals.

Terrarium

Set up a terrarium in an old aquarium or large glass jar. Get small plants from a nursery. Be sure there is sufficient drainage. Add a small lizard or toad when it's complete.

Dissolving

Have a small glass of water available. Put a spoonful of sugar in it and stir well. Take the spoon out and let everyone look at the water. Ask the children if they can see the sugar. Ask what they think happened to it. After several guesses, especially if someone says it disappeared, have one of the children taste the glass of water. It will taste sweet. Explain that the water tastes sweet because the sugar has dissolved not disappeared. Give glasses, sugar and spoons to children to duplicate the dissolving experiment.

Spoon Animals

Materials needed: plastic or wooden spoons (picnic variety), glue, construction paper and yarn. Have the children glue paper on the spoons to form whatever farm animals they wish. Use yarn for manes and tails of horses, whiskers of goats and tails of dogs and cows. Draw faces on the spoons with felt tip pens or crayons.

Paper Chains

This activity develops fine motor skills and it is fun and decorative as well. You will need to pre-cut strips of colored paper ½ x 4 inches. Demonstrate how to glue the pieces together and at the same time interlock them to form a chain. They are making **circles** of paper. Hang the chains around the room or from the ceiling.

SKILLS

Gluing

Learning to use glue is essential in doing arts and crafts projects. Have enough containers available so that each child has his own. You can keep refilling them from one large bottle. Stress that all you need is a small dab. A large glob will only make a mess and ooze around the object being glued. Make a collage gluing bits of torn paper onto another larger sheet.

Polishing Blocks

Use spray or liquid polish, soft cloths and natural wood blocks. Allow children to apply their own polish. Discuss how the polish makes the blocks shine and protects the surface. If you have any wood furniture, you may polish that too.

Washing Windows

If windows are accessible, let the children use spray cleaner and wash these. Windows too far away? Wash a mirror or someone's car windows.

Peeling Carrots

Learning to use a vegetable peeler is an interesting experience. Use large carrots and a flat vegetable peeler. Demonstrate how a person always peels **away** from the body. Allow the children to take turns with the peeler. When finished, cut the carrots into strips and dip in sour cream dip for the day's snack! Or, you can use them in the recipe on the following page.

FIELD TRIPS

Farms

For city children, farm animals are as exotic as wild ones. A farm is very exciting to children, especially if there are some animals they can pet, feed or hold. Be sure to watch the cows being milked and pigs being fed. Collect eggs in the hen coop if possible, and notice the machinery.

Making Butter

½ pint cream
1 clean jar with lid

Pour cream into jar and close lid. Children can take turns shaking the jar. After butter forms, pour off buttermilk and slightly salt. Spread on **square** saltines or **circle** Ritz crackers.

TO LEARN

Scrambled Eggs

A visit to an egg farm makes an excellent field trip and offers a chance to get very fresh eggs for this activity. You will need an electric skillet, some milk, eggs and bread for toasting. Discuss with the children where eggs come from and have them describe some ways in which eggs are fixed. Sometimes we eat them alone, and sometimes we put them in cakes, bread and quiche.

Mix: 6 eggs
      ⅓ cup milk

Put in a skillet that has been lightly greased. Stir while cooking to scramble. Salt lightly and serve on toast **triangles.**

TO LEARN
continued

Carrot Raisin Salad

5 to 6 carrots
1 cup raisins
½ cup mayonnaise

Grate carrots into a large bowl. Add the raisins and mayonnaise. Stir until mixed. Refrigerate until ready to eat.

Sunrise Sandwiches

4 whole, unsliced hamburger buns
4 eggs
margarine
4 slices cheese
salt and pepper

With a biscuit or cookie cutter, cut a 1-inch deep hole in the center of each bun, but not through the bottom. Carefully lift out the circle with a fork and butter the inside of the opening. Place buns on a cookie sheet and drop an egg into each hole. Sprinkle with salt and pepper. Bake in a 325° oven for 25 minutes. Top with cheese slices or grated cheese. Bake 5 additional minutes until cheese is melted and serve immediately.

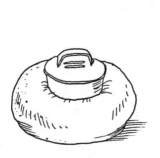

Ginsburg, Mira. **The Chick and the Duckling.** New York: Macmillan Publishing Co., 1972.
> A duckling and a chick hatch and the chick follows the duckling around until the duckling decides to go for a swim.

Kraus, Robert. **The Trouble with Spider.** New York: Harper & Row, 1962.
> Spider goes house hunting for a new home so he can invite the fly and ladybug for tea, but the solution to a new house is different than expected.

Kurtz, Mary DeBall. **Little Chick's Story.** New York: Harper & Row, 1978.
> Little Chick asks Broody Hen for a story, and gets a very special story because it is all about Little Chick.

Langstaff, John. **Over in the Meadow.** New York: Harcourt Brace Jovanovich, 1957.
> This introduction to numbers explores the activities of ten animal mothers and their babies.

Lenski, Lois. **The Little Farm.** Ithaca, NY: Walck & Rikhoff Bookpeddlers, 1970.
> Farmer Small is very busy with the daily and seasonal farm chores, from plowing to collecting eggs.

Podendorf, Illa. **The True Book of Animal Babies.** Chicago, IL: Childrens Press, 1955.
> The story of how various baby animals are cared for—including lambs, kittens, robins, lion cubs and alligators.

Williams, Garth. **The Chicken Book.** New York: Delcorte Press, 1946.
> In rhyming pattern, five little chicks learn from their mother how to make their wish for something to eat come true.

Number the babies from 1 to 6
To help mother hen care for her chicks.

PETS

PETS

Vocabulary

Pet, cage, aquarium, feed, veterinarian, dog, cat, hamster, gerbil, parakeet, canary, fish, turtle, pet shop.

All About Animals

On the class bulletin board or flannel board, put pictures of a number of animals, both zoo animals and those kept as pets. (Inexpensive sets of these paper pictures can be purchased at teachers' supply houses.) These pictures can be used over and over again to stimulate discussion and teach visual discrimination. Here are some examples of some of the questions that can be asked:

Which has the longest tail?
Which has the shortest tail?
Which has no tail at all?
Which ones have wings?
Which ones have hooves?
Which ones have scales?
Which ones lay eggs?
Which ones are found in a zoo?
Which ones make good pets?
Which one do you have for a pet?
Which one would you like to have for a pet?

Recognizing Voices

A tape recorder is a lot of fun. An inexpensive cassette recorder will come in very handy in the classroom. Children love to hear their own voices. You can interview each child on tape and then the children can have fun listening to themselves. Talking about their pets or the pets they would like to have would be a good topic of conversation.

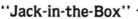

"Jack-in-the-Box"

"Jack-in-the-Box
So quiet and still,
Won't you come out?
Of course, I will!"

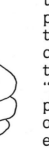

(Hand is closed into a fist with the thumb tucked inside. When the poem reaches the final line, "pop" the thumb up. Then have the children crouch down and pretend to be the jack-in-the-box. They can "pop" up by jumping up at the appropriate time. Try putting a face on the thumb with a pen for added fun!)

Sorting Colors

For sorting colors, sizes and shapes, use a large peg board with large pegs (four colors is sufficient to start). Put one peg of each color at the beginning of four separate rows on the board. Place all other pegs in a container. The children sort the colors by drawing pegs from the container and placing them in the appropriate row.

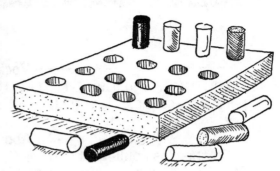

Provide different items for the children to sort (coins, silverware, buttons, ribbons, nuts and bolts, screws, blocks). They can classify the items according to size, color or shape.

Variation I: Color code the bottom of several Styrofoam meat trays and place them in the center of the table. Give each child a pair of scissors and a magazine. Cut out and sort pictures of colors.

Variation II: Get a round container that has divisions in it. (An old Tupperware relish container is perfect.) Paint each section a different color. Collect items that are the same color and place them in the container. Have students classify and sort objects by placing them into the correct corresponding color wedge section.

Feed the Birds

Bird feeders can be made from milk cartons. Assist children in cutting holes in the sides of the carton. Cover it with self-adhesive paper and attach a string for hanging. The children will enjoy putting the seed in the bottom of the feeder. The bird feeders can be taken home and tied from a tree.

Bug House

Make a bug house—it's easy! Fill an aluminum pie pan with plaster of Paris. While the plaster of Paris is still "gooey," sink a cylinder of wire or plastic screen into it. Let set. A lid for the bug house can be another pie plate. Add a small twig or two and you've got a nice house for a praying mantis.

Doggie in the Window

Obtain a recording of the song "How Much Is that Doggie in the Window?" Let the children sing the song along with the record. Then they can cut out pictures of dogs from magazines and glue them on white construction paper. Around the picture of a dog, have the children draw the front of a pet shop with the dog in the pet shop window. Or, the picture may be glued onto a tongue depressor and used as a stick puppet to move to the music.

Pet Store

There may be a pet store near you that would welcome a small number of children. The owner could show the children all the things people can buy to keep their pets well groomed and healthy.

Veterinarian

Pets get sick just like people. When they are sick they must see a special doctor called a veterinarian. Children can visit a veterinarian's office and see where the animals are treated.

Animal Shelter

Most towns have an animal shelter or Humane Society where animals are brought for adoption. Your local shelter may have guided tours or may send a person to your school to show a film on the work of the shelter and tell the children how to care for pets.

Paper Bag Puppets

Cut out the head shapes of pets—dog, cat, horse, bird, fish or hamster, and paste them on paper bag bottoms to make puppets. Bags should be small-sized and the kind that have a rectangular, flat bottom. Children can decorate the animal heads with crayons, paper or yarn. They may want to try talking to each other as the animals, or they may like to make up short plays.

Place Mats for Pets

Children will enjoy making a place mat to go under their pet's feeding dish. Take a piece of lightweight cardboard of a light color, and cut it into a 9 x 14 inch piece. (Posterboard and oak tag work very well for this.) Have the children draw a picture of the pet on the cardboard. You can help write the pet's name beside the picture. Then cover the whole thing with a piece of clear self-adhesive paper so the mat can be cleaned by wiping with a damp cloth.

COOK

TO LEARN

Peanut Clusters

1 cup sugar
¼ cup margarine
⅓ cup evaporated milk
¼ cup crunchy peanut butter
½ teaspoon vanilla
1 cup rolled oats (uncooked)
½ cup Spanish peanuts

Mix sugar, margarine and milk in saucepan. Bring to rolling boil. Boil 3 minutes, stirring frequently. Remove from heat and stir in peanut butter and vanilla. Fold in oats and peanuts. Drop by scant tablespoonful onto waxed paper on baking sheet. Let stand until set.

Ting-A-Lings

1 package (12 oz.) semi-sweet chocolate pieces
4 cups Wheaties, Cheerios, Kix **or**
   1 cup Spanish peanuts
1 to 2 cups chow mein noodles

Melt chocolate in double boiler. Cool at room temperature. Gently stir in cereal or peanuts with chow mein noodles until well coated. Drop by tablespoonful onto waxed paper. Place in refrigerator until chocolate is set, dry and hard.

Potato Chip Cookies

1 cup sugar
1 cup butter or margarine
1 egg yolk
1 teaspoon vanilla
1½ cups flour
1 cup crushed potato chips
1 cup nuts (optional)

Mix all ingredients and form into balls. Press with fork to flatten. Bake 12 to 14 minutes at 350°.

Dennis, Wesley. **Flip.** New York: The Viking Press, 1941.
Flip is a frisky cat who tries to jump a stream like his mother, but cannot do it until something wonderful happens to him in a dream.

Devlin, Wende and Harry. **How Fletcher Was Hatched.** New York: Parents Magazine Press, 1969.
Fletcher, a hound dog, has his friends construct an egg for him so he can hatch out of it and impress his owner and all the people in town.

Gag, Wanda. **Millions of Cats.** New York: Coward-McCann, 1928.
An old man tries to choose the perfect kitten as a companion for his wife and can't make up his mind, so he brings them all home and lets the cats decide who should stay with them.

Hoff, Syd. **Lengthy.** New York: Putnam, 1964.
Lengthy, an extra long dachshund, dislikes his size, until he finds a way to use his length to capture some bank robbers.

Keats, Ezra. **Pet Show.** New York: Macmillan Publishing Co., 1972.
Archie's cat disappears on the day of the big pet show, so Archie uses his imagination and brings a most unusual pet.

Podendorf, Illa. **The True Book of Pets.** Chicago, IL: Childrens Press, 1954.
This book is designed to help a child understand his pet and its needs.

Whitney, Alma Marshak. **Leave Herbert Alone.** Reading, MA: Addison-Wesley Publishing Co., 1972.
Jennifer wants to be friends with the neighbor's cat, but everyone tells her to "leave Herbert alone" until one day she discovers a way to make friends with Herbert.

Zion, Gene. **Harry the Dirty Dog.** New York: Harper & Row, 1956.
Harry hates to take a bath, but when he gets quite dirty, no one recognizes him, which motivates him to get clean again.

BOOK LIST

Draw a line from each animal to its home.

Make an X on the animal you would most like to have for a pet.
What would you feed your pet?
Where would your pet sleep?

OCEANOGRAPHY

SEASHORE

NOTES

OCEANOGRAPHY/SEASHORE

Vocabulary

Sun, sand, seashore, shells, waves, camping, bedrolls, salt, tents, full, empty, loud, soft.

"Five Little Campers"

"Five little campers sitting in the sun,
The first one said, 'I'd like to have some fun.'
The second one said, 'Let's all go for a cool swim.'
The third one said, 'I want to be the first one in!'
The fourth one said, 'Let's jump into the pool.'
The fifth one said, 'Oh, my, the water's cool!'
'Oooooooo,' went the wind and in went the sun,
and the five little campers all began to run."

Have pictures of a beach bag, pail and shovel, picnic cooler, picnic jug, picnic basket, toy trucks, suitcase and beach umbrella available. Place each picture, one at a time, on a flannel board, and ask the children what might be carried in each item and what each item is used for.

"Here's a Ball"

"Here's a ball for Billy (form ball with both hands)
Big and soft and round:
Here is Billy's hammer
Oh, how he can pound! (make pounding motion)

Here is Billy's music
Clapping, clapping so; (clap hands)
Here are Billy's soldiers,
Standing in a row. (hold fingers up in a line)

Here is Billy's trumpet, (put pretend trumpet to mouth)
Tu-too! Tu-too! Tu-too!
Here's the way that Billy
Plays at Peek-a-boo!" (cover face with hands)

Loud and Soft

Children love to make noise. Ask the children if they would like to make noise with you. "Did you know that noise can be loud or soft?" "Let's make a loud noise!" Clap hands loudly. "Let's make a soft noise." Clap hands softly. Have the children imitate you without your giving a verbal direction. Then, give each child a turn at choosing either a loud noise or a soft noise. Have the child tell the class which noise he is demonstrating.

──────────────── **Full and Empty** ────────────────

In learning the concepts full and empty, the children will also b
developing pouring skills. Begin with a substance such as sand or salt
Children have more control over this type of medium than they woulc
have over a liquid. Have a bucket of sand, cups and a ladle available.
Demonstrate by holding the cup so that the children can see the sand inside of it. Say "empty" and show the empty cup. Use the ladle to fill the
cup with sand (level with a ruler). Say "full." Allow the children to take
turns at making the cup full and empty. Stress vocabulary.

Stacking Pop Sticks

Use a stopwatch while stacking pop sticks. Ask "How many did you
stack in one minute?" Use a flat surface and have enough pop sticks
available so that each child can stack some. Count the number of pop
sticks that each child piled in one minute. You might want to shorten or
lengthen the time to count various numbers. Later, you may want to
stack pop sticks on top of a jar. This takes a little more precision, and the
children are involved with horizontal as well as vertical balance.

Shapes Puzzle

Cut a number of different shapes
from thin cardboard. Use triangle,
circle, square, rectangle, ellipse and
pentagon shapes. Trace the shapes
on oak tag. Mix up the cutouts and
see how quickly the child can place
them in the correct outline. Talk
about the names of the shapes as
they are placed in the correct space.

Individual Counting Tray

Have available a Styrofoam meat tray for each child. Cut strips from
colored paper and glue them in place to divide the tray into five sections.
Write a number in each of the sections with a felt tip pen. Punch the
same number of holes in each section. Cut drinking straws into 3-inch
lengths. Give each child fifteen straw pieces. Have the child place the correct number of straws into the corresponding holes. Play a game by calling out a number and having the child place the correct number of
straws into the counting tray.

──────────────── **Reflecting Light** ────────────────

Purchase a dozen small, inexpensive pocket mirrors. On a bright, sunny day go outdoors and practice reflecting sunlight onto the walls of the
school. Explain to the children how the mirrors reflect the light—the
light hits the mirrors, bounces off and hits the wall. Learning to capture
and control the reflection can be tricky.

Magnetic Fishing

Tie a magnet to a string and attach the string to a stick. Go "fishing" among a group of metallic and nonmetallic items (paper clips, washers, rubber bands, keys, coins, screws). Then fish for larger items (chairs, toys, refrigerator).

SCIENCE
continued

Lever

Show a picture of a cat and mouse on a seesaw. Ask which is bigger. How does the mouse hold such a heavy cat up on the seesaw? Ask if a child could lift the teacher off the floor on a seesaw. Explain that a lever is a machine that helps to lift things. It makes lifting very heavy things easier. Cut out pictures from magazines to illustrate items that use the lever principle (bottle opener, tire jack, seesaw, crowbar, screwdriver). Place a ruler on a block. Pretend it is a seesaw. Place different objects on one end, and lift them up by pressing the ruler down with your hand on the other end. Emphasize that the kind of machine used as the ruler is on top of the block is called a lever.

"Row, Row, Row Your Boat"

"Row, row, row your boat
Gently down the stream.
Merrily, merrily, merrily, merrily
Life is but a dream."

(Children can use arms to pretend they are rowing a boat.)

Water Lily Pond

Divide a foam egg carton into twelve separate sections. Scallop the outside edges and paint each cup a different pastel color. Glue one section inside another to create water lilies. Cut leaf shapes from the egg carton and glue them to the bottom of the flowers. Fill a bowl or a large bucket with water. Float the lilies on the water.

Bottle Top Faces

Paint the tops of discarded bottle caps of fruit juice or cooking ingredients. Draw a funny face on the top of the cap with fine-point markers. Use felt scraps and yarn to make facial details. Cut a circle of cardboard the same size as the cap. Place the cap on the outside of your shirt, put the cardboard piece inside and pinch together. You now are wearing a funny-face pin!

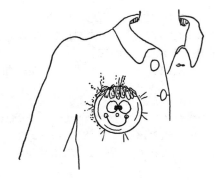

Underwater Flowers

Use a quarter to trace three circles on white paper. Cut different designs around the edge of the circles to suggest petals. Color each flower with a crayon. Cut three pieces of thread of different lengths, with the longest one being two inches long. Tape one piece of thread to each flower with waterproof transparent tape. Tape the loose end of the strings to a rock or other heavy object. Set the heavy object with the attached flowers in the center of a clear plastic drinking glass filled with water. Look at the beautiful flowers through the sides of the glass.

Different Rubbings

Take the children on a nature walk and bring sheets of thin, white paper and a large crayon. Look for different textured surfaces such as a brick or stucco wall, a cement sidewalk, gratings, an old piece of bark, a tree limb, a piece of wood or the trunk of a tree. Place the sheet of paper over the interesting textured surface and rub the paper with the crayon. Use a different sheet of paper for each rubbing. You can write the name of the object on the back of the rubbing. Children can show their collection of rubbings to their friends and have them guess what they were taken from.

continued

Fish Aquarium

Provide an empty gallon ice-cream container from an ice-cream store for each child. Cut a large oval opening in one side of the container. Have the child paint both the inside and outside of the container blue. Have children cut out fish and seaweed shapes from different colored construction paper. Tape a piece of clear plastic wrap to the opening of the ice-cream container. Glue the fish and seaweed to the inside of the container. Fill the bottom of the container with sand, and scatter seashells to complete the aquarium.

Aquarium Plate

Paint a sturdy paper plate blue. Cut out fish shapes, sea fans and seaweed from construction paper. Glue to the painted plate. Glue seashells and sand onto the bottom of the plate. Punch a hole in the top and use a length of yarn for a hanger.

─────────────── **Packing a Suitcase** ───────────────

Provide an empty suitcase for the children to use in the housekeeping area. Children love to pack and unpack for short vacations.

SKILLS

Funny Faces

Using ingredients on hand, have a funny face parade to celebrate the beginning of summer vacation. Mix food coloring with petroleum jelly and then finger-paint your face and arms. Talcum powder will make your face white. Watercolors can also be used on your face. Instant hair can be made from construction paper, newspaper or yarn. Cut a piece of construction paper into strips width-wise, leaving about an inch at the top. Tape the ends together and place your creation on top of your head. Trim the front (like bangs) so you can see, and place a funny hat on your head. News-papers can also be cut into strips, placed together and sewn on top with heavy thread. Tie a knot to hold the strips together and then spread the paper hair on your head. Trim the bangs so you can see. The ends of the paper hair can be rolled or twisted if you want curly hair.

Cut pieces of black or brown yarn to create a mustache, and tape it to the children's upper lips. Or, cut out a mustache from construction paper and tape it on.

An easy, instant scary monster can be created by using an old nylon stocking pulled over the children's heads. Don't forget old clothes, funny shoes or other clothes that are available in the housekeeping area of the classroom.

Popsicles

1 package (3 oz.) gelatin
1 envelope Koolaid (unsweetened)
1 cup sugar
2 cups boiling water
2 cups cold water

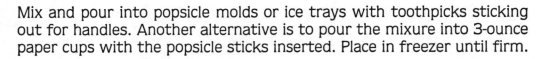

Mix and pour into popsicle molds or ice trays with toothpicks sticking out for handles. Another alternative is to pour the mixure into 3-ounce paper cups with the popsicle sticks inserted. Place in freezer until firm.

TO LEARN

TO LEARN

continued

Peanut Butter Balls

1 stick margarine
1 pound powdered sugar
2 cups crunchy peanut butter
3 cups Rice Krispies

Melt margarine and add other ingredients. Mix well. Form into balls and dip in chocolate mixture.

Mixture:
12-14 ounces sweet chocolate (or semi-sweet chocolate pieces)
⅓ bar of paraffin
Melt chocolate mixture together.

Place dipped chocolate balls on a tray and refrigerate until firm.

Honey Snacks

⅓ cup melted butter or margarine
⅓ cup brown sugar (packed)
¼ cup honey
3 cups natural cereal

Combine butter, honey and brown sugar. Mix over low heat until smooth. Pour over cereal. Firmly pack into a foil lined 9-inch square pan and bake at 450° for 6 to 8 minutes. Cool. Invert pan and cut into squares.

Ice Cream

½ cup sugar
¼ teaspoon salt
1 cup milk
3 egg yolks (beaten)
1 tablespoon vanilla
2 cups chilled whipping cream or evaporated milk

Pour into freezer can and put dasher in place. Cover can and adjust crank. Place can in freezer tub, fill tub ⅓ full of ice, add remaining ice with alternate layers of rock salt (6 parts ice to 1 part rock salt). Turn crank until it turns with difficulty. Draw off water and remove lid. Take out dasher and pack mixture down. Replace lid and repack in ice and rock salt. Let set several hours.

Popcorn Balls

One morning get out the popcorn popper or electric skillet and make popcorn. Children love to eat it and it's fun to watch. You can salt the popcorn and eat it or make popcorn balls.

2 quarts (8 cups) salted, popped corn
⅔ cup molasses
⅔ cup sugar
2 teaspoons butter or margarine
2 tablespoons vinegar
½ cup water
¼ teaspoon soda

Pick over the corn, discarding all hard kernels. Combine molasses, sugar, butter, vinegar and water in a saucepan. Boil gently, without stirring, until a little of the mixture becomes brittle when tested in cold water (270° on a candy thermometer). Remove from heat and stir in soda. Pour syrup over corn, mixing thoroughly. Let stand 5 minutes, then shape into balls. Makes 6 to 8 balls.

TO LEARN
continued

Oatmeal and More

2 cups cooked oatmeal
1 apple
2 cups milk
¼ cup brown sugar
½ cup raisins
½ teaspoon cinnamon

Cut apple into small pieces and add to cooked oatmeal. Add milk, brown sugar, raisins and cinnamon. Cook over low heat stirring often for approximately 10 minutes.

Pineapple Pistachio Perfection

1 small can crushed pineapple with juice
1 box instant pistachio pudding mix
1 8-ounce container nondairy whipped topping

Mix pineapple and pudding. Fold in whipped topping and mix well. Chill for 30 mintues.

Goudey, Alice E. **Houses from the Sea.** New York: Charles Scribner's Sons, 1959.

> The sights and sounds along the seashore are described with nice illustrations.

Lenski, Lois. **The Little Sailboat.** Ithaca, NY: Walck & Rikhoff Bookpeddlers, 1965.

> Captain Small and his dog Tinker spend a delightful day sailing, but hurry back to the bay to avoid a storm.

Lionni, Leo. **Fish Is Fish.** New York: Pantheon Books, 1970.

> A fable about a fish who takes a frog's advice on how to be happy just by being himself.

Lionni, Leo. **Swimmy.** New York: Pantheon Books, 1963.

> A clever little fish explores the beauty of the quiet ocean and discovers a way to enjoy it.

Lubell, Cecil and Winifred. **By the Seashore.** New York: Parents' Magazine Press, 1973.

> Discusses the characteristics of the shells and sea creatures found on the seashore.

Zion, Gene. **Harry By the Sea.** New York: Harper & Row, 1965.

> Harry the dog goes to the beach where he is caught by a wave, covered by seaweed and then thought to be a sea monster.

Find and circle three things plus one more. . .
That you would find along the seashore.

SEASONS

NOTES

THE SEASONS

Seasons, spring, summer, autumn, winter, climate, volcano, melt.

Heavy and Light

In order to experience the difference between **heavy** and **light**, the children can pretend to be scales. Demonstrate by standing with your arms extended from your shoulders horizontally. You are now a scale. Place a block in on hand and lower that arm. Say, "Heavy goes down," and at the same time, raise your other arm. Say, "Light goes up." Give all the children a turn at being a scale. Place blocks of varying weights in their hands and move their arms for them while using the words "heavy" and "light." Then let them show you on their own which arm is heavy and which is light.

Variation: Bring a small balancing scale to class. Experiment with objects found in the classroom. Let the children guess which ones will be heavy and which ones will be light.

If your playground has a teeter-totter, use it as a scale to find out who in the class is heavier than whom.

Letter Shapes

Before children can read, they must know that each letter is a symbol in itself and that these symbols are made up of straight and curved lines. Write some upper-case letters formed entirely from straight lines such as A-T-M-N-Z-E-F-H on the chalkboard. Have the children come to the board and trace over the letters while saying the word "straight." Then put up some letters with curves and have the children trace over these. It is not necessary to name the letters. It is only important that the children see the differences in them.

Writing Names

Children love to see their names in print. Print their names (in upper case) one at a time on the chalkboard. See if they can recognize their own names. "Do you know that your name has a shape?" Say the shape out loud and encourage the children to say it with you. For instance, "Gail" sounds like "curved, slanted, straight, straight!" Do this for each child's name and have the class repeat it.

Identifying Shapes

Put a variety of traceable items on a tray. Have the children close their eyes while you choose an item and trace it on a blank sheet of paper. Then return the item to the tray. Show the children the tracing and let them choose the item that was traced. Next, let the children be the teacher and, one at a time, select an item to be traced.

Fun With Shapes

Cut various colors of construction paper into the three basic shapes—circle, square and triangle. Hold up each shape and identify it by name. "This is a square." "This is a circle." Then, give the pile of shapes to the children and have them group the pieces according to shapes—all the  squares in one pile, and so on. When this is done, have the children sort the pieces according to color, no matter what their shape. Sorting may be a group activity or an individual one.

Melting

The snow melts when the sun shines on it. That is why snowmen don't last into the spring. Heat makes lots of things melt. Heat can come from many sources to melt objects. Put an ice cube in a pan on a hot plate and watch it melt. Put a piece of chocolate candy in the pan and watch it melt. Ask the children what they think would happen if you added more heat. Give the children a small piece of chocolate candy to put in their mouths and let melt. While they are doing this, light a small birthday candle and let it melt. Explain that when spring comes, the temperature of the air goes up, and the sun shines more so the snow will melt.

Volcanoes!

Discuss volcanoes. Explain that a volcano is a large rock-rimmed hole in the ground that shoots up fire, and the fire is so hot that it melts the rock. That's HOT! The melted rock is called "lava." Volcanoes do not occur everywhere, only in certain places in the world. Accompany this discussion with pictures, books or a film on volcanoes.

Build A Volcano

When baking powder is combined with water and vinegar, carbon dioxide is released. This can make a dandy volcano in the yard. Build a small mound of dirt and scoop out the top. Fill the hole with a tablespoon of baking powder. Mix ¼ cup vinegar with 1½ cups warm water and a little red food coloring. Allow the children to pour the mixture onto the baking powder. It erupts!

———————— Windy Weather Scarves ————————

Gather a collection of old silk scarves. (Ask mothers of students to donate some old ones.) Play a record that contains some flowing musical passages. Choose a variety, both slow and fast. Discuss with the children how the trees look when the wind is blowing slowly. Put the music on and let the children create dances, holding the scarves in their hands above their heads. Let them twirl and dip and make all sorts of pretty designs in the air.

Ice Statues

When the seasons change, the weather changes. In some parts of the world, it becomes cold enough to have ice and snow. In these places, people carve ice statues. Divide the children into pairs. The children are to "mold" their partner into an ice statue. Pretend it is very cold outside. The statues come to life and do a little dance with their partners. (A little music on the record player will do well here.) The children take the statues home to their warm houses. Once inside the houses, they begin to melt and become puddles on the floor. The children become sad. Start over again and this time reverse the children's roles.

———————— Snowstorm in a Jar ————————

Give the children paper punches and let them punch out a pile of white circles. Put the circles in a baby food jar full of water. After you fasten the lid on tightly, shake the jar and make a snowstorm inside!

Winter Mittens

Find soft scrap material, such as cotton balls, furry fabric or yarn. Have two mitten shapes pre-cut for younger children. Older children may draw and cut their own mittens from construction paper. Glue "soft" scraps on mittens. Punch a hole in the bottom of the mittens and fasten together with a 10-inch length of yarn.

continued

Arctic Rock Garden

It's a snow garden! It's easy to do and fun. Have the children collect some small rocks and scrub them. Pile them into a pie tin. Mix together:

4 tablespoons salt
4 tablespoons bluing
4 tablespoons warm water

Stir and dissolve the salt as best you can. Add 1 tablespoon household ammonia. Stir and pour mixture slowly over rocks, covering all surfaces. The garden will begin to grow in a few hours. A few drops of food coloring may be added if a colored garden is desired.

"Magic, Magic, see it grow. It looks like snow!
But don't touch it as it will crumble."
Note: Be sure to caution the children against putting the "snow" into their mouths!

Fashions for the Seasons

Get four large pieces of white butcher paper or four sheets of oak tag. At the top of each piece of paper, print the name of the season—SPRING, SUMMER, AUTUMN, WINTER. Have a supply of old catalogs from Sears, Penney's or Spiegel available. Have the children cut out pictures of clothes and glue them under the name of the season when they would most naturally wear them, bathing suits under summer, fur coats under winter and so on.

Pinwheels

Cut an 8-inch square of construction paper. Have the children cut on lines already drawn on the construction paper. Fold each end marked with an "X" to the center. Place a straight pin through the center and attach it to a plastic straw. Bend the end of the pin down and wrap with tape to protect the sharp point. Blow it, hold it in front of a fan or take it outside. Watch the pinwheel turn!

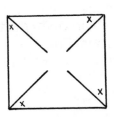

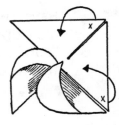

LIFE

SKILLS

Setting the Table

Set up a place setting using a plate, glass, napkin, knife, fork and spoon. Demonstrate how a table setting is correctly done. Leave your setting as an example, and let the children copy it one at a time with another set of dishes. Soon, they will be able to do it without an example to copy!

Do-Littles

¾ cup shredded coconut
¾ cup chopped dried apricots
½ cup seedless raisins
½ cup sweetened condensed milk
1¾ cups cornflakes

In a medium bowl, stir all ingredients except cornflakes. Cover and chill for 30 minutes. Put cornflakes in a plastic bag and squeeze to crush. Set aside. Roll coconut mixture into 1-inch balls. Toss each ball in crushed cornflakes to coat. Cover and store in refrigerator.

Banana Granola Cookies

½ cup butter or margarine, softened
1 cup firmly packed brown sugar
1 egg
½ teaspoon vanilla
1 cup mashed bananas (2-3 ripe bananas)
1½ cups all purpose flour
1 teaspoon cinnamon
½ teaspoon baking soda
½ teaspoon salt
1 cup granola

Cream butter or margarine and sugar. Add egg, vanilla and bananas and beat until well blended. Add flour, cinnamon, baking soda and salt. Mix well. Stir in granola. Drop by teaspoonfuls about 2 inches apart onto cookie sheets. Bake 12 minutes in 375° oven.

COOK

TO LEARN

Keats, Ezra. **The Snowy Day.** New York: The Viking Press, 1962.
A small boy wakes up one morning to find his first snowfall, and anticipates exploring this new world.

Podendorf, Illa. **The True Book of Seasons.** Chicago, IL: Childrens Press, 1955.
An explanation of why some parts of the Earth have changing seasons, and how living things adapt to these changes.

Scheck, Eleanor. **City in the Summer.** New York: Macmillan Publishing Co., 1969.
City summer activities center around a young boy's anticipated trip to the beach with an old man.

Scheck, Eleanor. **City in the Winter.** New York: Macmillan Publishing Co., 1970.
Jimmy is snowbound and has no school, so his grandmother provides different activities to keep him busy.

Schlein, Miriam. **Snow Time.** Racine, WI: Whitman Publishing Co., 1962.
Making snowballs or a fort, sliding on a sled or just watching snow fall, are a few of the activities one can do when it snows.

Tressett, Alvin. **Autumn Harvest.** New York: Lothrop, Lee & Shepard, 1970.
Fall arrives and various activities occur—harvesting crops, leaves turning, watching the stars of Orion's belt.

Tressett, Alvin. **Johnny Maple Leaf.** New York: Lothrop, Lee & Shepard, 1948.
A story about a leaf from the time it is a bud to when it turns yellow and dry.

Tressett, Alvin. **White Snow, Bright Snow.** New York: Lothrop, Lee & Shepard, 1947.
A beautiful picture story of the snowflakes' silent fall and how the world looks covered with snow.

Wildsmith, Brian. **Seasons.** New York: Oxford University Press, 1980.
Beautiful pictures accompany the story of how different animals react to the different seasons.

Zion, Gene. **Really Spring.** New York: Harper & Row, 1956.
When spring was late in coming, the townspeople decided to make their own spring with some interesting results.

Zion, Gene. **The Summer Snowman.** New York: Harper & Row, 1955.
Henry keeps a snowman in the freezer and surprises everyone on the Fourth of July.

Draw a line to match each picture with the name of the season.

SPRING   SUMMER

WINTER   FALL

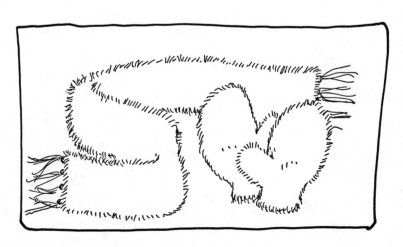

RAINY DAY

NOTES

RAINY DAY

Vocabulary

Rain, thunderstorm, lightning, rainbow, umbrella, mushroom, goggles, museum, fashion show.

Tall and Short

Sit on the floor with the children. Using blocks, boxes or other stackables, build a small city with both tall and short buildings. Use your hand as a descriptive tool. Raise your hand up high along the tallest building and say "tall." Put your hand on the top of the shortest building and say "short." Build three buildings and describe them as "tall, taller, tallest." Do the same with "short, shorter, shortest."

Measuring Tall and Short

Compare the heights of the children by making marks on the chalkboard. Use two of the children at a time, and let the rest of the class decide who is tall and who is short. Do it again using three children and use the terms "tall, taller, tallest."

"Open, Shut Them"

"Open, shut them, (open and shut fingers)
Open, shut them,
Give a little clap, (clap)
Open, shut them,
Open, shut them,
Lay them in your lap. (put hands in lap)

Creep them, creep them, (walk fingers up arms toward face)
Creep them, creep them,
Right up to your chin,
Open wide your little mouth,
But do not let them in." (close mouth and shake head)

"Where is Thumbkin?"

"Where is Thumbkin? Where is Thumbkin? (thumbs tucked into fists)
Here I am! (hold up one thumb)
Here I am! (hold up other thumb)
How are you today, sir? (wiggle one thumb at the other)
Very fine, I thank you.
Run away, run away." (hide hands behind back)

This is to be sung to the tune of "Frère Jacques." Now sing it over with all the rest of the fingers: "Pointer," "Tall Man," "Ring Man," "Pinky."

Touchable Counting Poster

Collect some interesting small objects that are alike. You will need ten of one object, such as buttons, nine of another object such as paper clips and so on. On a large sheet of posterboard, draw ten evenly spaced lines about two inches apart across the page. Neatly draw the numeral 1 on the first line and glue one object on that line to go with it. Put the numeral 2 on the second line and glue two small objects on that line. Continue writing numerals and gluing objects until you reach the numeral 10. The poster will help children who need to touch objects while they count. It will also help them see at a glance the fact that eight is more than two.

Take Home Number Posters

Children can make take home number posters similar to the one on the class bulletin board. On a piece of 8 x 10 inch construction paper, make ten lines and write a numeral on each line. Let the children glue objects in the correct lines. Here are some suggestions for inexpensive items to glue: ten inked thumbprints, nine navy beans, eight pieces of rice, seven reinforcement circle stickers, six small pieces of colored ribbon, five paper clips, four buttons, two peanut shells, and a smiley face sticker.

Sorting by Size and Color

The teacher may buy attribute shapes in a set from an educational supply house or cut a set from construction paper. There should be large and small squares, triangles, rectangles and circles. There should be four colors: red, blue, green and yellow. You can put the shapes in a pile on the floor and ask the children to select all the shapes which are "large and blue," "small and yellow," or whatever combination you choose. In this way, children learn to consider two attributes when selecting the shape. Older children may enjoy selecting a shape that has three attributes, such as the "large, red, square."

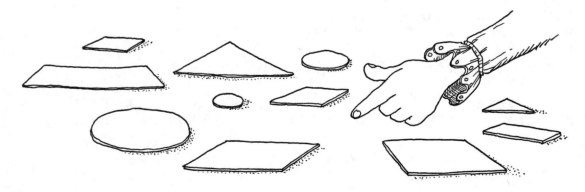

Mailman House Match

Put a variety of pictures of houses on the bulletin board. These can either be cut from magazines or made from construction paper. Beneath each house, put an envelope with a number on it. Numbers may have one or more digits, depending on the age of the child doing the activity. The child who plays "mailman" carries a pouch or sack containing cards or "letters" which have numbers that correspond to the ones on the board. The child then delivers the letter to the correct house by matching the numbers, and placing the card in the envelope.

continued

How Flowers Drink

When it rains, the flowers, trees, grass and other plants get a drink. How do they drink? The water goes up the roots, through the stem, to the leaves. Get a stalk of celery and a white carnation. Put each in a jar with water. Tell the children that red food coloring will be added to the water so they can see the water going up the stem to the leaves. Check the clock and see how long it takes for the water to reach the petals and leaves.

Plastic Bag Fun

A plastic bag can be a lot of fun and provides an interesting way to show some scientific principles. Let each child be responsible for one "experiment," and let the others in the group tell what the results of the experiment are.

• Put some apples in the bag. What happens to the bag? Does it change shape? What shape does it take?
• Put some water in the bag. What shape does it take now?
• Poke two holes in the bag filled with water. What happens to the bag? What happens to the water?
• Fill a new bag with air and hold the end tight. A bag filled with air can hold something up. Find something you can set on the bag that the bag will hold up. Now let the end go and see what happens.
• Fill the bag with air again and secure the end with a rubber band. Now try to submerge it in a sink filled with water. What happens?

SCIENCE
continued

Take Apart

Often more emphasis is put on building or putting together than on taking apart. This is not to be confused with destroying! Have a few old household appliances available that can be taken apart using a few simple tools such as pliers, screwdrivers or a wrench. Be sure to tell the children that these are old appliances that do not work any more. Also, stress that no appliance should be taken apart unless it is **unplugged.** This activity will improve motor skills and give the children something to do on a rainy day.

Fashion Show

Invite the children to take part in a fashion show. Make a block stairway leading to the stage. Use the doll corner for the dressing room. You be the announcer and describe each child's outfit as he comes on stage to model. Some children may choose to model their own clothes instead of dressing up.

Raindrop Pictures

Give the children large pieces of white construction paper and water base paints, either watercolors or tempera. Let them make pretty designs on the paper with a variety of colors. Then, take the pictures outside to the edge of the porch and hold them out in the rain. Watch the raindrops hit the paper and cause the paint to run and smear together. Bring the pictures in and let them dry.

Clay Porcupine

Take a ball of clay and shape a snout on one end. The rest can be left an oblong shape. Use two beans for eyes. For the spines, cut plastic or paper drinking straws (the thin ones) into various lengths. Be sure to cut them on a slant so the ends will be sharp. Stick the straws all over the body of the porcupine, excluding the face. Put it on display for the class to enjoy.

Paper Punch

This activity affords practice in manual dexterity and creativity. Have small squares of colored paper available. (Origami paper is very good for this purpose.) Practice folding the paper into halves and quarters. Now, demonstrate the use of the paper punch. Children can punch holes all over the quartered paper and then open it up to see the pattern it makes.

Goggles

You can look at the world through rose colored glasses, or any colored glasses you like, with a few simple materials. Using construction paper or lightweight cardboard, cut out goggles for the children. Leave the eyeholes empty until the children have a chance to pick the colored cellophane they want to use. Glue the cellophane circles to the inside of the goggles and add string for tying. How strange the world looks when it is a different color!

--- **Trips** ---

Rainy days are great times for taking indoor field trips to interesting places. Some places to go that are fun and informative are:

A shoe repair shop Watch the cobbler repair a pair of shoes.

A florist Find out how a florist makes those pretty corsages and bouquets.

A dry cleaners What happens to your clothes when they are sent to the cleaners?

A beauty shop or barber shop Watch all the people getting their hair cut and styled.

--- **Snickerdoodles** ---

¾ cup margarine or butter
1 cup sugar
2 eggs
¾ cup milk
2 teaspoons baking powder
2½ cups flour

Mix well and drop by teaspoonfuls onto a greased cookie sheet. Sprinkle with sugar and nutmeg and put a raisin on each cookie. Bake at 375° approximately 10 minutes.

Forgotten Cookies

2 egg whites, room temperature
⅔ cup sugar
½ cup nuts

Heat oven to 350°. Beat egg whites very stiff. Add sugar a little at a time. Fold in nuts. Drop by teaspoonfuls onto ungreased cookie sheet. Place in oven and shut oven door. Turn oven off. Leave the cookies in oven overnight. Do not open oven door until morning.

Barlett, Margaret Farrington. **Where Does All the Rain Go?** New York: Coward, McCann & Geoghegan, Inc., 1973.
> Explains how the rain cycle works, and what effects it has on us.

De Paola, Tomie. **The Cloud Book.** New York: Holiday House, 1975.
> Introduces ten of the most common clouds and the myths that have been inspired by their shapes.

Forte, Imogene. **Rainy Day—Magic for Wonderful Wet Weather.** Nashville, TN: Incentive Publications, Inc., 1983.
> Outdoor activities to help children get in touch with nature, indoor experiments and opportunities for finding answers to rainy day questions.

Ginsberg, Mirra. **Mushroom in the Rain.** New York: Macmillan Publishing Co., 1974.
> A mushroom provides a safe place for an ant and other forms of animal life during a rainstorm.

Hillert, Margaret. **Run to the Rainbow.** Chicago: Follett Publishing Co., 1981.
> Three children, searching for the rainbow, see many colorful objects.

Schlevitz, Uri. **Rain Rain Rivers.** New York: Fauer, Melvin, Sussman & Sugar, 1969.
> A little girl sits in her attic bedroom during a rainstorm and lets her imagination take her to places that the rain touches—the city, streams and sea.

Schnick, Eleanor. **Rainy Sunday.** New York: The Dial Press, 1981.
> This book is about a little girl who tells how she feels about everything around her on a rainy Sunday afternoon.

Tressett, Alvin. **Rain Drop Splash.** New York: Lothrop, Lee & Shepard, 1946.
> An explanation of how raindrops form a puddle which grows into a pond, then a lake, and then a river which finally joins the sea.

Yoshima, Taso. **Umbrella.** New York: The Viking Press, 1958.
> A little girl hopes for a rainy day so that she may use her new red rubber boots and big blue umbrella.

Keep a record of this month's rainy days by drawing a cloud on the calendar each time it rains.

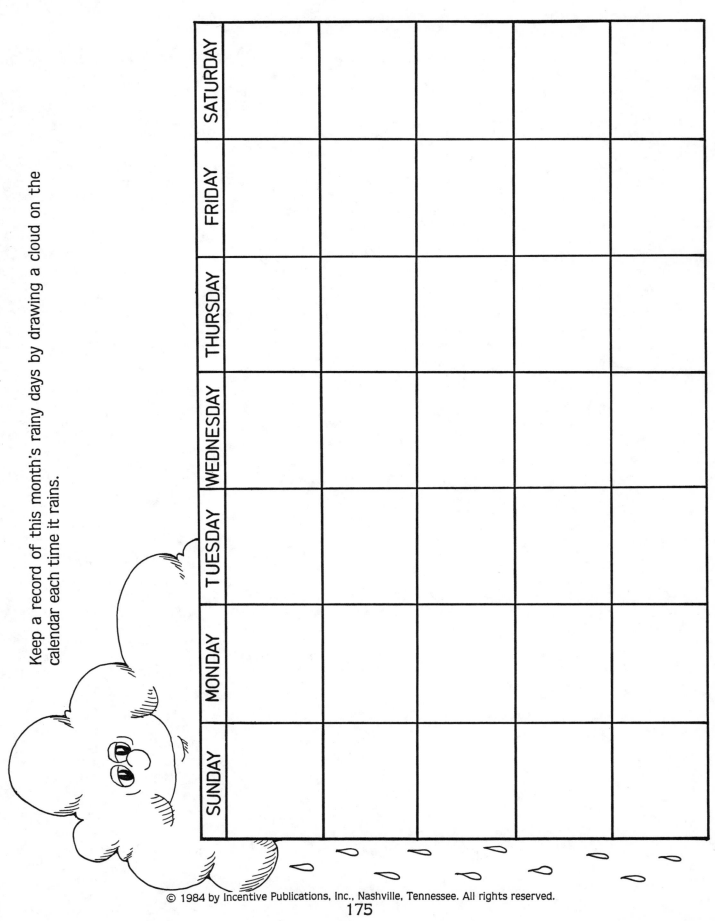

SUNDAY	MONDAY	TUESDAY	WEDNESDAY	THURSDAY	FRIDAY	SATURDAY

HALLOWEEN

NOTES

HALLOWEEN

----------- Vocabulary -----------

Pumpkin, witch, goblin, ghost, cat, broom, spider, web, top, little, bottom.

Halloween Analogies

Form a group to play a word game. Give a sentence and the children have to guess the correct missing word. Different words may be stressed.

1. Apples are red, pumpkins are _____.
2. Pilots fly in planes. _____ fly on broomsticks.
3. Birds build nests. Spiders spin _____.
4. Eyes are found at the top of the face. A mouth is found at the _____.
5. Witches wear black. Ghosts wear _____.
6. Angels are seen at Christmas. Goblins are seen at _____.
7. The stem is found on top of the pumpkin. Seeds are found in the _____.
8. A boy's best friend is a dog. A witch's best friend is a _____.
9. On Christmas, we go caroling. On Halloween, we go _____ or _____.
10. Pumpkins have seeds in the middle. A jack-o'-lantern has a _____ inside.

Prepositions

Use a bean bag or a small block for a preposition. You should have a small table and a bag for demonstration purposes. Seat the children on the floor. You should then give the bean bag to one of the children and tell her "please put the bean bag **on** the table." Then ask another child to put the bean bag **under** the table. Continue using the prepositions **on, under, in, over, between, behind, beside.** The game can be made more interesting by making a few "mistakes" to test the children and keep them on their toes.

----------- "Five Little Pumpkins" -----------

"Five little pumpkins, sitting on a gate . . .
The first one said, 'My, it's getting late'
The second one said, 'There are witches in the air'
The third one said, 'I don't care'
The fourth one said, 'Let's run, run, run'
The fifth one said, 'Oh it's just Halloween fun'
Ooooooh, went the wind . . . Out went the lights,
And the five little pumpkins rolled out of sight."

FINGER PLAY
continued

MATH SCIENCE

"Three Little Witches"
"One little, two little, three little witches
Fly over haystacks, fly over ditches,
Slide down the moon without any hitches,
Hi, Ho, Halloween's here!"

——— Matching Numerals I ———

This activity gives the children an opportunity to match numerals 0-10 and to name them. Use two sets of number cards from 0-10. These can be made with index cards and markers. Let the children assist you in setting up one set of numerals in sequence. Say the numeral names several times. Let the names flow in a natural rhythm—they should be appealing and fun! Now, put the other set of numerals into a bucket. Each child, in turn, draws a numeral from the bucket, names it and matches it to its mate in the sequence. Continue until everyone has had a turn.

Matching Numerals II

Use your double numeral set 0-10 to do some backward matching. Begin by lining up one set of numerals in sequence and naming them again. This is to refamiliarize the children with the numeral names. Now distribute this numeral set, one numeral to each child. Use the other numeral set as a model for matching. Put them into a bucket and shake to mix. Tell the children to close their eyes while you draw a numeral from the bucket and place it under a cup. With their eyes open, the children must try to see if their numerals match the model in the middle as you uncover it and recover it quickly. This quick action lends to the excitement of the game. Then put the numeral back into the bucket and draw again.

——— The Jack-O'-Lantern ———

Cut out the top of a pumpkin. Have the children remove the seeds and pulp from inside. Place a lighted candle in the pumpkin and replace the cut-out top. After a few minutes, remove the top and have the children look inside. They will "discover" that the candle will not stay lit without air. Then, cut a jack-o'-lantern face into the side of the pumpkin and relight the candle. Emphasize the need for oxygen in order for a flame to stay lit.

Seeds in Fruits and Vegetables

Select an assortment of fruits and vegetables (try a tomato, cucumber, orange, apple, peach or apricot, banana, grapefruit, bean). All these fruits and vegetables must be fresh, not frozen or canned. Open the fruits and look for the seeds. Explain how seeds contain the beginnings of a new plant and that plants make fruit so there will be more plants. Stress that the seeds in fruit can be planted and new plants will grow from them. Let the children plant seeds from a pumpkin and tomato in small boxes filled with fertilized earth. Be sure the fruit is very ripe when the seeds are removed. Discuss how some seeds are eaten (tomato, banana) while others are too large and hard to be digested (peach, orange). Sometimes the seeds are called "pits" or "stones."

──────────────── **Halloween Pumpkin** ────────────────

Materials: lots of newspaper, large grocery bags, dark construction paper, orange tempera paint, yarn, paste.

Have the children stuff grocery bags with newspaper. Tie the top of the bags with yarn to form stems. Paint the bags orange. Make facial features out of construction paper and paste them on the bags. Younger children can paste pre-cut facial features on the bags.

Cat Masks

continued

Materials: black construction paper, white pipe cleaners, tongue depressor.

Cut out an outline of a cat face from construction paper. Make sure the eyeholes are large enough to see through. Staple the tongue depressor to the middle of the mask, then tape the pipe cleaners to the front of the mask to form whiskers. Use the masks at "rug time" when saying the finger-play "The Five Little Pumpkins." Exchange the words "five little pumpkins" with "five little black cats."

Shape Pumpkins

Materials: orange construction paper, yellow and black triangles, squares and circles already cut, or paper from which to cut them.

Cut a round shape from orange paper for the pumpkin. Cut two triangles for eyes. Cut one square for the nose. Cut six or more circles for the mouth. Glue the eyes at the top, the nose in the middle and the circles at the bottom to make a face. Younger children can work with pre-cut shapes. This activity is a good one to teach shapes and also top, middle and bottom concepts.

continued

Halloween Spiders

Materials: egg carton "cup," black tempera paint, pipe cleaners, popcorn, yarn.

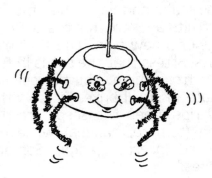

Paint the pre-cut egg carton "cup." Punch holes for legs. Insert pipe cleaners through the holes. Bend the legs and secure with tape. Glue on popcorn "eyes." Attach a piece of yarn to the top for hanging. Children can hang them in a huge spider web made from black angora yarn, hanging from the ceiling.

Witch of Shapes Airplane

Materials: black, white and yellow construction paper, one straw, paste, stapler.

You should fold a 9 x 12 inch piece of black construction paper in half lengthwise with each half folded again (like an airplane) to form the witch's body. Draw a circle face. Cut it out and paste it on the end of the witch's body. Draw and cut out a triangle nose. Paste it on the face. Draw a triangle hat. Paste it on the witch's head. Draw and cut out a square for the end of the broom. Staple the straw on the witch's body and the square end on the straw for the broom. You now have a witch who flies!

Bread Dough Pumpkins

Materials: bread dough, paint, string, varnish, tin foil.

Recipe for dough: 1 cup salt, 4 cups flour; add water until dough is pliable.

Give students small balls of dough. Have them make jack-o'-lanterns. Pat the dough flat and poke a hole at the top. Place on a cookie sheet and bake at 300° for 3 hours. Paint with tempera paint and varnish. Paste on triangles of black felt for facial features. Put a string through the hole for a necklace.

Rhythm Band

Children enjoy rhythm and music and the activity of marching around the room. If musical instruments cannot be purchased, inexpensive handmade ones can be just as much fun. The following instruments are simple and easy to make from common household items.

- dowel sticks make excellent drumsticks and rhythm beaters
- pie plates are wonderful cymbals
- potato chip cans with a handful of beans inside make great maracas
- sandpaper stapled to wood blocks makes interesting sounds
- rubber bands stretched over paddles, boxes or pieces of cardboard
- old jingle bells tied together
- coffee cans with plastic lids make wonderful drums
- the body as an instrument (clapping hands, stamping feet, mouth noises)

Guitar Strumming

A guitar tuned to the "C pentatonic" scale provides a pleasant accompaniment to such songs as "Frère Jacques" and "Row, Row, Row Your Boat." Children can strum the open strings themselves. They should know however, that the guitar is tuned a special way for these songs.

Toasted Seeds

Wash seeds taken from a ripe pumpkin and let dry. Place on a cookie sheet and salt. Cook in 400° oven turning often until brown (10 minutes). Or, place seeds with 2 tablespoons of oil in a frying pan. Cook until seeds are lightly brown. Sprinkle salt over seeds.

Pumpkin Muffins

1 egg
½ cup pumpkin cooked
½ cup oil
1½ cups flour
½ cup milk
2 teaspoons baking powder
½ teaspoon salt
½ teaspoon cinnamon
½ teaspoon nutmeg
½ cup raisins

TO LEARN

Set oven at 400°. Grease muffin tin or use paper baking cups set inside muffin tin. Beat egg. Stir in milk, pumpkin and oil. Measure flour by dip method. Stir in dry ingredients. Batter will be lumpy. Fill cups ⅔ full. Bake 20-25 minutes.

COOK

TO LEARN
continued

Spooky Sweets

Have a parent volunteer bring baked cupcakes or sugar cookies to class. Have the children ice the cupcakes or sugar cookies (use orange or chocolate frosting). Decorate to resemble black cats, witches or goblins with licorice, candy corn, gumdrops, raisins, chocolate chips or sprinkles.

Pumpkin Cake

Bake a cake in a round layer pan. Tint the frosting orange by adding red and yellow food coloring mixed together, or by purchasing orange food coloring. Border the cake, and draw on a broad smile with chocolate coconut. Use candy corn for the teeth and eyes and licorice for a stem.

Other Food Favorites

Bobbing for apples in a giant tub, eating marshmallows dangling from strings in a doorway or finding hidden peanuts in shells are Halloween party favorites.

Caramel Apple Surprise

1 bag of caramels
several apples sliced into bite-size pieces

Melt caramels in double boiler with a bit of water over low heat. Scoop into a bowl. Let the children use toothpicks to dip apple pieces into warm caramel.

Witches' Brew

1 quart apple cider
4 cinnamon sticks
12 whole cloves
¼ teaspoon nutmeg
1 quart chilled ginger ale

Combine cider, cinnamon sticks, cloves and nutmeg in saucepan and bring to a boil. Simmer 10 minutes and strain. Chill. Pour in serving bowl and add ginger ale.

Borten, Helen. **Halloween.** New York: Thomas Y. Crowell, 1965.
> A story describing the customs of Halloween today and how Hallow-een came to be from its origin in European countries.

Bright, Robert. **Georgie's Halloween.** New York: Doubleday Publishing Co., 1958.
> Georgie, the shy ghost, tries to work up enough courage to join the village Halloween party.

Cooper, Paulette. **Let's Find Out About Halloween.** New York: Franklin Watts, 1972.
> An explanation of how Halloween is celebrated in different countries and how Halloween is celebrated in America.

Hellsing, Lennart. **The Wonderful Pumpkin.** New York: Antheneum Publishers, 1976.
> Little Bear and Big Bear plant a pumpkin seed that grows so big they decide to make a house out of it. The house takes them on many adventures around the world.

Lasson, Robert. **Which Witch?** New York: David McKay Co., 1959.
> A "picture book about two witches, a rich witch and a witch with an itch."

Prelutsky, Jack. **It's Halloween.** New York: Greenwillow Books, 1977.
> Written in rhyme, various activities that are a part of Halloween—skeletons, ghosts, black cats, haunted houses—are delightfully phrased and illustrated.

Riley, James Whitcomb. **The Gobble-uns'll Get You Ef You Don't Watch Out!** Philadelphia, PA: J.B. Lippincott Co., 1975.
> An illustrated version of James Whitcomb Riley's famous peom about Little Orphan Annie.

Stevenson, James. **That Terrible Halloween Night.** New York: Green-willow Books, 1980.
> Louis and Mary Ann try to scare Grandpa on Halloween night, but they don't succeed because of what happened to Grandpa when he was their age. He tells them why through a story of his experience one Halloween night.

Thayer, Jane. **Gus Was a Friendly Ghost.** New York: William Morrow & Co., 1962.
> Gus shares a vacant summer home with his friend the mouse, until the owner's return causes some trouble.

Only one of the five witches matches the shadow.
Circle the correct witch.
Color the other witches.

Use black, orange and yellow
To discover a funny fellow.

black   1
orange 2
yellow 3

THANKSGIVING

NOTES

THANKSGIVING

Vocabulary

Wattle, gobble, roast, sauce, dressing, stuffing, Pilgrim, Mayflower, worship, thankful, cranberries, cornucopia, harvest, old, young, time.

Make Up a Story

Explain to the children that a good way to tell a story is to decide on three basic things—a character, an object and a setting where the story takes place. Have available pictures of a turkey, Pilgrims and Indians, the Mayflower and a table filled with food. Have students take turns giving their version of the first Thanksgiving.

Developing a Sense of Time

Time is a difficult concept for children to understand and therefore a lot of experience is necessary in order for time awareness to be developed. Ask children:

1. What do you think was here before the school was?
2. What do you think has changed since you have been at this school?
3. Who is the oldest person you know and how old is he?
4. Who is the youngest person you know and how old is he?
5. How old do you think this building is?
6. How old is the house you live in?
7. If there are plants in the room, ask the children how old they think the plants are?

Take the children outside and talk about the age of such things as the school building, the houses, parked automobiles, the trees, grass, birds, flowers, rocks and clouds.

Kinds of Clocks

Have the children describe various kinds of clocks we use to tell time. Have a wristwatch, pocket watch, wall clock, clock radio, alarm clock and stopwatch in a paper bag. Take them from the bag one at a time, and demonstrate the uniqueness of each. Listen to each clock and note the difference in tempo. Ask the children, "What time is it when you go to bed? What is it like outside? What time do you get up in the morning? What time do you eat breakfast, lunch and dinner? What time do you go to school?" Relate other events that the children participate in to the hour in which they occur.

Variation: Have the children close their eyes and hide a clock that has a loud ticking sound. Choose a child and have him locate the hidden clock. Children will enjoy taking turns locating the clock.

MATH SCIENCE

FINGER PLAY

"Clap 2, 3, 4"

"Clap 2, 3, 4, 5, 6, 7, (clap hands)
Snap, 2, 3, 4, 5, 6, 7, (snap fingers)
Shake, 2, 3, 4, 5, 6, 7, (shake hands)
Slap, 2, 3, 4, 5, 6, 7, (slap knees)
Roll, 2, 3, 4, 5, 6, 7, (roll hands around each other)
Tap, 2, 3, 4, 5, 6, 7, (pound fists)
Push, 2, 3, 4, 5, 6, 7, (push hands)
Clap, 2, 3, 4, 5, 6, 7." (clap hands)

Shape Creatures

Have different sizes of four different shapes available (circles, squares, rectangles and triangles). Place the assorted shapes into separate boxes (one for each shape). Talk about the names of the four different shapes. Have each child make a shape creature by gluing pieces of one basic shape to a piece of paper. Have the child give a name to the creature he has created and write it on the bottom of the paper.

Bowl and Beans

Have a plastic margarine bowl and five beans for you and each child. Have everyone place all five of the beans under their bowl. You lift your bowl and remove four beans and place them on top of the bowl and ask, "How many beans do I have left under my bowl?" When a child answers correctly, you can respond that four from five leaves one. Have the students repeat this statement. The children can take turns removing beans from under their bowls, and asking the others how many are left.

Clock Game

Have the numbers 1-12 painted on large circles of oak tag or posterboard. Place the numbers in a large circle to represent a clock. Have the children hop around the clock calling out the number they hop on—"two o'clock, three o'clock," and so on.

Pine Cone Feeder

Loop a long wire around a large pine cone or tie a length of yarn around the cone to form a hanger. Spread peanut butter into the spaces of the pine cone. Press the pine cone into a pan of wild bird seed (purchased in the pet section of a grocery store). Hang the cone from the eaves of a building or from a tree, and watch our bird friends enjoy a banquet.

Recognizing What Things Are Made Of

Invite the children to play a guessing game with you. Say, "A window—what's it made of? A table—what's it made of? A slipper—what's it made of?" Take items made out of different substances (cup, fork, toy car, pop can) out of a paper bag and ask the children to tell what the item is made of—wood, glass, rubber, stone, cement, fabric, plastic or metal. Place all the items made of the same substance in separate piles. After all the items have been sorted and classified, have the children tell the name of each item and what it is made of before placing it back into the bag.

—————————— "The Pumpkin Ran Away" ——————————

(to the tune of "The Farmer in the Dell")

"The pumpkin ran away
  2nd verse—cranberry
  3rd verse—turkey
  4th verse—bread
Before Thanksgiving Day
Said he, they'll make a pie with me
  2nd verse—sauce
  3rd verse—roast
  4th verse—stuffing
If I decide to stay."

"A Funny Bird!"

(sung to "Row, Row, Row Your Boat")
"The turkey is a funny bird
His head goes wobble, wobble,
And all he says is just one word . . .
Gobble, Gobble, Gobble!"

—————————— Thanksgiving Plate ——————————

Paint a paper plate with any color of tempera paint. Talk about the different foods that are eaten during Thanksgiving—turkey, stuffing, cranberries and pumpkin pie. Go through old magazines and cut out pictures of the food you would like to have on your Thanksgiving dinner plate. Glue the pictures to the plate. Write "My Favorite Thanksgiving Dinner" at the bottom. Poke a hole through the top of your plate and tie on a yarn hanger. Make sure to stress the different food groups and see that your dinner is balanced.

Turkey Hands

Place the child's hand on a piece of paper and trace around it. Finish the turkey by adding a wattle and feather details. Color in the feathers and other features.

SCIENCE
continued

MUSIC ART

continued

TO LEARN

Turkey Mobile

Bend a wire coat hanger into a circular shape. Cover the hanger shape with a nylon stocking. Cut eyes, beak, wattle, feet and feathers from construction paper and glue these on. Use yarn to hang the turkeys around the room.

Pilgrim Village

Use a large grocery box or a large box lid as a base. Paint the base brown with tempera paint. Make tepees from twigs and brown paper (grocery sacks can be used). Tape tepees to base. Log cabins can be made by covering small cardboard boxes with popsicle sticks. A thatched roof can be made from grass or crepe paper strips. Add cut out trees, bushes and cornstalks. A fence can be made from sticks too. Figures can be fashioned from construction paper or from pipe cleaners.

Cornucopia Centerpiece

Make a large cone from a large piece of brown wrapping paper. Use either tape or staples to hold the cone together. Trim the large open end and curl the pointed end over with your hand. Paint the outside of the cornucopia with brown tempera. Crumple colored tissue paper into balls to resemble fruit—yellow for lemons and bananas, orange for oranges, pink for peaches and red for apples. Tissue paper can also be colored with a felt tip pen for variations in fruits. Make tiny balls for grape clusters and tape them together. Add leaves and vines made from green paper. Glue the fruit in the mouth of the cornucopia. Or, cut pictures from seed catalogs or magazines and glue in the mouth of the cornucopia.

Pumpkin Bread

Place the following dry ingredients in a large bowl:
1½ teaspoons nutmeg
4½ cups sugar
5¼ cups flour
1 teaspoon cinnamon
1½ teaspoons salt

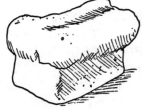

Make a well in the middle of dry ingredients and add:
6 eggs
1 cup water
1½ cups oil
3 cups cooked pumpkin

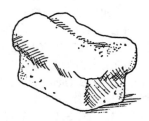

Blend well. Pour batter into well-greased soup cans ½ full, or small individual loaf tins. Bake at 350° for one hour. Makes 12 to 14 small loaves.

Orange Turkey Boats

Cut oranges in half, scoop out the pulp and mix with can of whole-berry cranberry sauce. Spoon mixture into orange rind which forms the turkey's body. A radish or cherry tomato on a toothpick makes the turkey's head. Carrot sticks, celery tops, or green onion stalks can be added for the tail feathers.

COOK
TO LEARN
continued

Pilgrim's Mayflower Boats

Dissolve 1 3-ounce package of cherry gelatin to 1 cup boiling water. Add to 1 can whole-berry cranberry sauce. Chill until thickened. Fill a peach or pear half with the mixture. Use a carrot shaving on a toothpick as a sail and stick in the boat shell. Chill in refrigerator until gelatin mixture is firm.

Cranberry Delight

1 can whole-berry cranberry sauce
1 8-ounce container nondairy whipped topping
2 bananas
1 box raspberry flavored gelatin

Mix raspberry gelatin with whipped topping. Add cranberry sauce and sliced bananas. Mix well and chill for 30 minutes.

Turkey Salad

2 cups chopped turkey
2 tablespoons mayonnaise
1 tablespoon sweet pickle relish
⅛ cup chopped celery

Mix ingredients together and serve with tomatoes or on toasted English muffins.

Balian, Lorna. **Sometimes It's Turkey, Sometimes It's Feathers.** Nashville, TN: Abingdon Press, 1973.
> Mrs. Grimm finds a turkey egg, hatches it, and then takes care of the turkey in anticipation of Thanksgiving dinner—but something unusual happens.

Bartlett, Robert Merrill. **Thanksgiving Day.** New York: Thomas Y. Crowell, 1965.
> The story of the Pilgrims and how a family celebrates this holiday.

Dalgliesch, Alice. **The Thanksgiving Story.** New York: Charles Scribner's Sons, 1954.
> The story of the first Thanksgiving in America.

McGovern, Ann. **The Pilgrim's First Thanksgiving.** New York: Scholastic Book Services, 1973
> This story takes the reader from the Pilgrims' decision to leave England through the first Thanksgiving feast in the New World.

Gibbons, Gail. **Thanksgiving Day.** New York: Holiday House, 1983.
> Presents information about the first Thanksgiving and the way that holiday is celebrated today.

Sandak, Cass R. **Thanksgiving.** New York: Franklin Watts, 1980.
> The Pilgrims left England and settled in a new land. They celebrated their second winter with a feast that is now an American tradition.

Shopp, Martha and Charles. **Let's Find Out About Thanksgiving.** New York: Franklin Watts, 1964.
> An explanation of how Thanksgiving came to be and why Americans celebrate it.

Showers, Paul. **Indian Festivals.** New York: Thomas Y. Crowell, 1969.
> An explanation of how various Indian tribes celebrate various Indian holidays with sacred customs of days past.

Williams, Barbara. **Chester Chipmunk's Thanksgiving.** New York: E.P. Dutton, 1978.
> Chester Chipmunk wants to share his Thanksgiving dinner with his cousin and some friends. For differing reasons, only Oswald Opossum could come. Then, something exciting occurs.

Wyndham, Lee. **Thanksgiving.** Champaign, IL: Garrard Publishing Co., 1963.
> The history of the holiday and how we celebrate it today is explored.

Color the three turkeys that are in their own space.
Circle the turkeys that are out of place.

CHRISTMAS

HANUKKAH

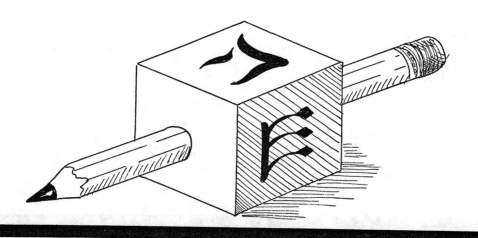

NOTES

CHRISTMAS

--- **Vocabulary** ---

Santa, elf, sleigh, reindeer, North Pole, Christmas tree, candle, stable, manger, star, Wise Men, shepherd, gingerbread, decorate, snowflake.

Story Acting

Christmas is a perfect time for storytelling and dramatics. Read a favorite Christmas story to the children. The next day, play a tape recording of you reading it again. This time the children can act out the parts. Discuss with each child how the character would act, and practice for a few moments. Let the children trade parts and do it again.

The public library probably has records of Christmas stories. Borrow a few and let the children act these out after listening to them.

--- **Evergreens** ---

Collect an assortment of evergreens, including two kinds of Christmas tree branches. Pass these around for the children to see, touch and smell. Use the following questions for discussion:

Why are they called "evergreens"?
How are their leaves different from other leaves?
How are they the same as other leaves?
Do they have a smell?
Why do people use these trees as Christmas trees?
Where do people get their Christmas trees? (tree lots, woods, artificial ones from a store)
Are some of them sharp and prickly?
Are some of them smooth and soft?
How do you decorate your tree at home?

Pine Cones

Pass around a pine cone.
Where does a pine cone come from?
What does it do? (seed for new pine tree)
Does it have a smell?
What color is it?
Give some words that tell about it. (describe it)
What would happen if we planted it in the ground?

Holly, mistletoe, poinsettia—these are other traditional Christmas plants. Use the same questioning techniques with these as were used with the evergreens.

WARNING!! Mistletoe leaves, holly berries and poinsettia leaves and flowers are POISONOUS. Be sure to tell this to the children. They are NEVER to put these in their mouths. Have children wash their hands after handling the plants.

FINGER PLAY

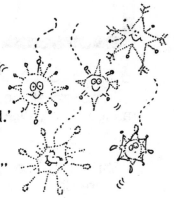

"Five Little Snowflakes"

"Five little snowflakes dancing on the wind,
The first one said, 'It is fun to twist and spin.'
The second one said, 'There is winter in the air.'
The third one said, 'But we don't care!'
The fourth one said, 'We will tumble to the ground.'
The fifth one said, 'Decorate the woods and town!'
Whoo went the wind in the cold winter night,
And the five little snowflakes whirled out of sight."

Singing Carols

There are many lovely songs for the Christmas season. If a piano and pianist are not available, get some Christmas records from the library or from the children themselves. Some easy songs:

Sacred—"Away in a Manger," "Silent Night," "Carol of the Drum."
Secular—"Frosty the Snowman," "Santa Claus is Coming to Town," "Up on the Housetop." (This last one has some nice hand movements.)

Rudolph Reindeer

Materials needed: two shades of brown construction paper, red construction paper, white paper for eyes and black crayons.

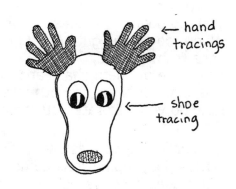

← hand tracings

← shoe tracing

Have one child put her shoe on the lighter brown paper, while another child traces the outline of the shoe. Have the children trace their own hands on the darker brown paper. Cut out all the patterns and glue as illustrated. Use red for the nose and white with black for the eyes. The eyes and nose may be pre-cut for younger children.

Spinning Spirals

Materials needed: inexpensive paper plates, paint or glitter, glue, string.

Starting from the outside edge, cut the plate in a spiral. Decorate with paint or glitter and hang from the small center disk. They're beautiful when hung from the classroom ceiling!

Styrofoam Cup Bells

Wire two Styrofoam cups together with ribbon or yarn. Glue on glitter, sequins, foil stars, rickrack, lace or any other things you have handy. Cut saw teeth or scallops around lips of cups and decorate the cups with glitter. To hang, punch a hole in center of the cup bottom. Cut a length of ribbon or yarn, fold in half, then insert the ends through the hole in the cup bottom and tie a knot.

Tree Garland

White Styrofoam packing "krinkles" make a nice tree garland alone or combined with other things. Using a large-eyed needle strung with yarn or string, poke a hole through the "krinkle" and string like popcorn. You can alternate krinkles with pieces of drinking straws cut in 1-inch lengths or small star shapes cut from colored construction paper.

continued

Helping Hands Wreath or Tree

Materials needed: green construction paper and scissors.

Have the children trace around their hands on the green paper. Cut out the "hands." Curl "fingers" around a pencil. Staple the hands to the bulletin board in the shape of a wreath or tree. Use brown paper for the trunk. The wreath or tree may be decorated with circles cut from old Christmas cards. Staple these "ornaments" on.

Pine Cone Ornaments

Materials needed: pine cones, white tempera paint mixed with soap flakes, glitter, paintbrushes and yarn.

With a brush, coat the tips of the pine cone "petals" with the white paint mixture. Sprinkle glitter on the edges of the cone and shake the excess off. Tie a piece of yarn to the top of the cone and hang the ornament on the tree.

Paper Gingerbread Boys

Materials needed: brown construction paper, white hole reinforcements, miscellaneous white trim.

Have the children cut out the shape of a gingerbread boy which has been drawn or dittoed on brown paper. Decorate the boy with paper reinforcements and other miscellaneous trims.

continued

Glitter Ornaments

Materials needed: waxed paper, white glue, two feet of brightly colored yarn, glitter.

Dip the yarn in glue, wiping off the excess with your fingers. Arrange the yarn in abstract patterns on the waxed paper, being sure to have the yarn overlapping in many areas. Let it dry overnight and carefully lift it off the waxed paper. Apply glue followed by glitter or sequins.

Easy Bulletin Board Tree

Materials needed: large sheet of white butcher paper, green tempera paint, small pieces of a household sponge, old Christmas cards, Styrofoam packing "krinkles."

Cut the white paper in the shape of a large tree. Have the children paint the tree by dipping sponges in the paint and wringing them out. Dabbing on the paint creates a nice textured effect. Hang the tree on the board and decorate it with shapes cut out of old Christmas cards. Or, you may want to glue on Styrofoam bits to represent snow.

Wall Hangings

Materials needed: brown burlap (12 x 14), shapes cut from various pieces of felt, glue, thick brown yarn used for wrapping gifts.

Glue a black 4-inch length of construction paper over the width edge of the burlap. Punch two holes 3 inches from each side. Knot a 14-inch length of yarn through the holes. Glue pieces of felt on burlap.

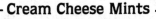

Cream Cheese Mints

2 ounces cream cheese (room temperature)
½ teaspoon oil of peppermint
1⅔ cups powdered sugar
red or green food coloring

Mash cream cheese, add flavoring and coloring. Mix in sugar. Knead with hands until like pie dough. Roll in balls the size of marbles. Place on side in small amount of sugar. Press sugar side in mold. Unmold at once. Molds can be purchased at a cake decorating supply house.

204

Gingerbread Men

⅔ cup butter or margarine
1½ cups granulated sugar
⅓ cup molasses
2 eggs
5 cups flour
2 teaspoons baking powder
½ teaspoon baking soda
1 teaspoon ginger

In large bowl, cream butter and sugar. Stir in eggs and molasses. Sift dry ingredients and add to mixture. Knead with hands until a smooth ball of dough forms. Roll out on a heavily floured surface. Roll to ¼-inch thickness and cut with cookie cutter or by hand. Place on greased cookie sheet and bake in 400° oven for 8 to 10 minutes. When cool, decorate with white frosting. Makes approximately 24 cookies 4 inches high.

COOK
TO LEARN
continued

Unbaked Chocolate Cookies

4 cups sugar
1 stick margarine
½ cup cocoa
1 cup milk

Cook all ingredients for 1 minute at a hard rolling boil. Remove from heat and add the following:

4 cups oatmeal
1 cup peanut butter
1 package coconut or nuts
1 teaspoon vanilla

Drop by spoonfuls on waxed paper and refrigerate.

Christmas Eggnog

1 egg
1 cup milk
1 tablespoon sugar
½ teaspoon vanilla
dash salt
nutmeg

Beat egg. Add milk, sugar, vanilla and salt. Beat well with egg beater. Sprinkle nutmeg on top.

HANUKKAH

Vocabulary
Star of David, menorah, shamas, dreidel, latkes.

Tell the children the story of Hanukkah. Discuss the meaning of the Hebrew letters used on the dreidel and how the game is played. Explain other ways this holiday is celebrated by Jewish families.

Egg Carton Dreidel
Materials: Styrofoam or cardboard egg cartons, pencil or pointed dowels, felt tip pens or crayons.

Cut a cup from the bottom of a Styrofoam or cardboard egg carton. Cut deeply into the cup to make four pointed petals. Insert a sharpened pencil or pointed dowel through the bottom of the cup. With a felt tip pen, add one of the Hebrew letters on each of the four sides.

———— Potato Pancakes—Latkes ————

5 large potatoes with skins
2 eggs
½ teaspoon baking powder
1½ tablespoons flour
1 teaspoon salt
¼ cup fresh parsley
1 slice onion

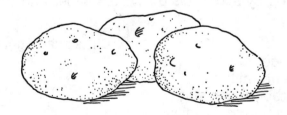

Wash potatoes and cut into 1-inch cubes. Heat a greased griddle or frying pan. Put eggs, baking powder, flour, salt, parsley and onion in a blender. Add ½ cup of the potato cubes. Cover and blend on high. Remove the cover and gradually add the rest of the potatoes, taking care not to overblend. Pour mixture onto the greased griddle. Brown on both sides.
Makes 10 large latkes if poured by ¼ cup or 50 small ones if poured by the tablespoonful.
Serve hot with applesauce or sour cream.

Adler, David A. **A Picture Book of Hanukkah.** New York: Holiday House, 1982.
> Discusses how the celebration of Hanukkah came about, what it signifies and ways in which it is celebrated today.

Behrens, June. **Hanukkah.** Chicago: Childrens Press, 1983.
> The sights, sounds and meaning of this holiday are explained with color photographs.

Branley, Franklin. **The Christmas Sky.** New York: Thomas Y. Crowell, 1966.
> In this book, the story of the Wise Men's journey to Christ's birthplace and the many theories astronomers have attributed to the star that led them are discussed.

Coopersmith, Jerome. **A Chanukah Fable for Christmas.** New York: G.P. Putnam's Sons, 1969.
> A little Jewish boy dreams about presents, trees and stockings on Christmas. As he is dreaming, someone dressed in red appears. What do you think happens next?

Drucher, Malka. **Hanukkah—Eight Nights, Eight Lights.** New York: Holiday House, 1980.
> Introduces history, customs, rituals, food, games and gifts associated with the Festival of Lights. Recipes, puzzles and crafts are included.

Eaton, Anne Thaxter. **The Animals' Christmas.** New York: The Viking Press, 1972.
> Stories and poems about the Christmas holiday.

Gibbons, Gail. **Christmas Time.** New York: Holiday House, 1982.
> A brief look at why and how we celebrate Christmas

Greenfield, Howard. **Chanukah.** New York: Holt, Rinehart and Winston, 1976.
> The historical significance of Chanukah is explained and how it came to be celebrated.

Hurd, Edith. **Christmas Eve.** New York: Harper & Row, 1962.
> A "reverent retelling of the part the animals played on the eve that Christ was born."

Keats, Ezra. **The Little Drummer Boy.** New York: Macmillan Publishing Co., 1968.
> A young boy joins a group of people going to Bethlehem, but is too poor to bring a gift and instead, offers the Baby something else.

Color and cut out the shapes at the bottom of the page.
Use them to decorate the Christmas tree.
Can you name all the shapes?

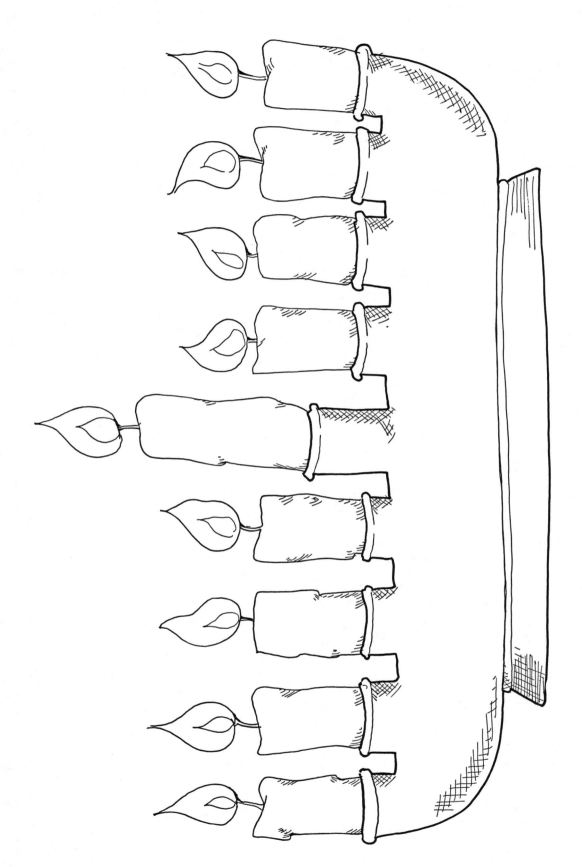

Number the candles on the menorah.
The candle in the center is called the shamas.
Can you tell how many candles are on each side of the shamas?

VALENTINE'S DAY

NOTES

VALENTINE'S DAY

Vocabulary

February, love, giving, valentine, Cupid, heart, bow and arrow, sweetheart.

Right and Left

Find some way to decorate children's shoes so that the right one is different from the left one. Use string, bows, colored labels or anything that is easy to see and can be taken off. Let the children practice putting their right foot forward and then putting their left forward. After they have gotten used to which is right and which is left, remove the items and see if they can remember which is which. The next day do the same activity with the hands, tying ribbons around the wrists.

Predicting

This is a good activity to encourage logical thinking and verbal expression. It is done in three parts: first the question, then the action, then the conclusion. For instance, "What will happen if I drop this stone into this bowl of water?" Children give predictions. You or a child then demonstrate. Then the children are asked to verbalize the conclusion. "It fell to the bottom and it got wet." Some suggestions:

What happens if I put a cork in water?
What happens if I put sugar in water?
What happens if I drop this rubber ball?
What happens if I push the swing and then let go?
What happens if I put this cup of water in the freezer?
What happens if I put this drop of food coloring into the bowl of water?

How Do They Go?

This is a simple exercise and one that can be enjoyed by even the youngest members of the class. Start with familiar barnyard animals and ask, "How does a duck go?" (quack, quack). "How does a turkey go?" (gobble, gobble). Move on to jungle animals. "How does a lion go?" (roar!). Then another day you can use vehicles—"How does a fire engine go?" or household appliances, "How does a vacuum cleaner go?" Try a different set of things each day.

Weighing

A bathroom scale can be used to weigh many things—from a baby brother to five cans of pineapple juice. Assemble a number of items and let the children take turns weighing them. Help them look at the numbers and determine how much each of them weighs. A baby scale works well and a digital scale is also fun. Weigh an object on two or more scales to see if it weighs the same amount on both. Even if the children cannot read the numbers correctly, they will develop an understanding of how a scale is used.

More Weighing

If there is a supermarket nearby, take a walking field trip through the produce department. They have wonderful scales there to weigh oranges, apples and all sorts of things. The scales are also very easy for children to read. Let children experiment weighing produce.

Weighing Friends

Make a weight chart for the children in the class. Let each child weigh a friend on a bathroom scale and you can write the weight on the chart. Every month have a weigh-in so the children can see how much they've grown.

Bulbs

Not all flowers grow from seeds. Some grow from bulbs. Bring examples of seeds and bulbs to class. Let the children examine them with their fingers, eyes and a hand lens. Then ask, "How are seeds and bulbs alike?" "How are they different?" Seeds can then be planted in old coffee cans with drain holes in the bottom. Many bulbs will grow well in a shallow pan filled with an inch of smooth rocks and water. A glass pan is great for this because the children can pick it up and see the roots growing.

Cuttings

Not all flowers grow from seeds or bulbs. Some grow best from cuttings. Bring some of these cuttings to class and explain how most are started in water and then transferred to soil. Chrysanthemums and roses are good for this. Your local nursery may be willing to give you a few cuttings to use in class. Start them growing in a clear jar and watch the roots develop.

─────── **Salty Hearts** ───────

Mix the following ingredients together in a large bowl:

4 cups salt

1 cup water

1 cup liquid starch

Divide the mixture among several small bowls or margarine tubs. Color each with a different color tempera paint. Give the children a plain white paper heart and let them paint as desired.

A Bookmark for Your Valentine

Cut small sections from a paper doily and red and pink hearts from construction paper. Small pictures of flowers may be cut from a seed catalog too. Glue these pictures to a strip of construction paper. When dry, cover the pictures with clear self-adhesive paper. Punch a hole in the narrow end and put a piece of yarn or ribbon through it. Trim the edges with pinking shears to give a nice effect!

Valentine Card Holder

For this activity, you will need two inexpensive white paper plates. Cut the first one across the top to resemble a valentine. Cut the second one across the middle the same way. Decorate the plates with children's names and hearts, old valentines, red rickrack, yarn and glitter. Staple the second plate onto the first one with the bottom edges together. Punch a hole in the top and hang with string.

Here's My Heart Necklace

Bend a red pipe cleaner into the shape of a heart. Glue it onto a piece of white construction paper. Let dry. When dry, cut away the paper outside the heart, write the child's name in the heart with a red felt tip pen and punch a hole in the top. Hang with yarn around the child's neck. This can also be done with a white pipe cleaner on red paper.

King and Queen of Hearts Crown

Cut a piece of red paper 1½ inches wide and long enough to go around the child's head. Staple the ends together. Cut two strips of pink paper 1 inch wide and 18 inches long. Staple these to opposite sides of the headband, crisscrossing them. Decorate with cut-out hearts, pieces of old valentines or valentine heart candy.

continued

Queen of Hearts Tarts

1 cup flour
⅓ cup plus 1 tablespoon shortening
2 tablespoons water
pinch of salt

Cream the flour and shortening together. Add the water and salt and mix well. Roll into small balls. Press down into muffin tins with your fingers. Bake 8 to 10 minutes at 350°. Cool and fill with strawberry jam or cherry preserves and top with a spoonful of whipped topping.

It would be nice if the children were familiar with the nursery rhyme before baking the tarts. They might even want to try some creative dramatics by acting out the poem.

Valentine's Cookies

No time to bake or no oven? Go to the store and buy some inexpensive plain sugar cookies. Whip up a batch of regular white icing, tint it pink and let the children have fun decorating the cookies. Add some red sprinkles and a few candy hearts, and they'll be works of art!

Heart of My Heart Pizza

Follow the directions on a packaged pizza mix, but roll the dough out into a heart shape. Create a Valentine's Day message with pieces of cheese or by writing in the tomato sauce.

TO LEARN

Balian, Lorna. **A Sweetheart for Valentine.** Nashville, TN: Abingdon Press, 1979.
>The people of St. Valentine village discover a large baby on the steps of the town hall. Because she is so large, the villagers decide to take care of her as a group.

Brown, Marc. **Arthur's Valentine.** Boston, MA: Little, Brown & Co., 1980.
>Arthur has a secret admirer and gets teased by his classmates when they find his valentines.

Bulla, Clyde Robert. **St. Valentine's Day.** New York: Thomas Y. Crowell, 1965.
>An explanation of how valentines began, how the holiday was celebrated and how Valentine's Day is celebrated today.

Cohen, Miriam. **Bee My Valentine.** New York: Greenwillow Books, 1978.
>Jim is excited about sending and receiving valentines at school, but a classmate receives only a few cards, so the class works together to make him feel better.

De Paola, Tomie. **Things To Make and Do for Valentine's Day.** New York: Franklin Watts, 1976.
>Activities and things to make for Valentine's Day.

Guifoile, Elizabeth. **Valentine's Day.** Champaign, IL: Garrard Publishing Co., 1965.
>This book tells how Valentine's Day has changed from the Roman days of St. Valentine, to the symbols and customs used today.

Hayward, Carolyn. **A Valentine Fantasy.** New York: William Morrow and Co., 1976.
>A tale of how Valentine's Day came into existence and how the heart became its symbol.

Krahn, Fernando. **Little Love Story.** Philadelphia, PA: J.B. Lippincott Co., 1976.
>Getting to the heart of a Valentine gift becomes a major project, but the reward is well worth it.

Help Cupid find his way to the Valentine's Day party.

Color one heart red.
Color one heart pink.
Cut and paste the two hearts together (back to back) for a special valentine treat.

EASTER

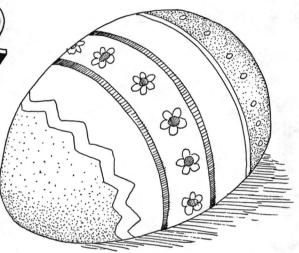

PASSOVER

NOTES

EASTER/PASSOVER

Vocabulary

Rabbit, egg, hatch, pretzel, Seder, matzo, fasting, moror, charoses, circle, rectangle, triangle, square, Lent.

Passover

After 430 years of slavery under the cruel Pharaohs of Egypt, the Jews were finally freed. Moses, their leader, guided them to the new land God had promised them. Passover is a celebration of this historic event. Matzo is an important part of this holiday. The Hebrews left Egypt so fast that there wasn't time to let the bread rise. Today Jewish families use matzo in remembrance of this journey.

Seder

The traditional family dinner, called the Seder, commemorates the Passover event and the approach of spring. Parents and children read aloud from the Haggadah the story of the Jews' exodus from Egypt. The Passover platter contains different foods that symbolize the Exodus. Have a sample platter available to show the children the different foods present at a Seder meal.

Matzo: Represents the hardship of the long flight from Egypt when the Hebrews had to bake their bread in the hot, desert sun.

Parsley: Represents a sign of spring and new life. It is dipped into a small bowl of salt water as a remembrance of the tears of slavery.

Moror: (bitter herbs): Horseradish which represents the bitterness of slavery.

Charoses: Represents the bricks and mortar the Hebrews used to build the Pharaoh's cities and monuments while they were slaves in Egypt.

Lamb Bone: Represents the sacrificial lamb.

Roasted Egg: Represents the survival of the children of Israel and is another sign of spring.

Wine Glass: An extra glass of wine is placed on the table, and the door is opened for Elijah the prophet to come with news of freedom everywhere.

LANGUAGE

continued

MATH

How the Pretzel Came To Be

In early Christian times, many people did not eat milk, eggs or fat. They did this during Lent to show religious devotion. This was called fasting. So in order to make bread, only flour, salt and water were used. The dough was rolled into slender ropes and then shaped like two arms crossed in prayer. The Germans later changed the word for crossed arms to "brezels." From brezels we get the modern-day word of pretzel. Pretzels, for hundreds of years, were eaten only during Lent, but during the 1800s people began to eat the crossed-arm bread all year round. Today, we have several kinds of pretzels—the hard, crisp pretzels and the larger, soft pretzels made popular by the Pennsylvania Dutch.

How the Easter Egg Came To Be

The most important holy day in the Christian calendar is Easter, and it is celebrated in different countries in different ways. The coloring of Easter eggs began with the ancient Egyptians. Coloring eggs is a happy family activity.

——— Matching Shapes ———

Draw a circle, square, rectangle and triangle on a piece of cardboard, and color them solidly with one color. Cut some shapes from oak tag. These shapes should be smaller than the shapes on the cardboard and they should vary in size and type. Make some rectangles narrow and others wide. Make sure to include equilateral, isosceles, scalene, obtuse, acute and right triangles. Children need to be made aware of the other kinds of triangles besides the equilateral. Put the cut-out shapes into a container and match the shapes to the shape board. Remember to point out that a square can also be a rectangle. If the children have difficulty in recognizing the triangles, point out that a triangle has three sides and three corners. Have children use the correct vocabulary as they match the oak tag shapes with the shapes on the cardboard.

Hatch an Addition Chick

Place different amounts of lima beans or other marking devices inside plastic eggs. Some eggs may have just one bean inside, some may have two beans inside, some up to five beans inside an egg. Mix the eggs and place them in front of the children. Tell a child to choose two eggs and to open them. Then ask how many beans are in the first egg and then the second egg. Than ask how many beans would there be if you added the first number to the second number. Give each child a turn to hatch an addition egg.

Sitting on Shapes

Use four large cardboard shapes (circle, square, rectangle, triangle). Put them in a row across the floor. The object of the game is for one child to sit on one shape and for the other children to guess which shape is missing. Whoever guesses first is "it" next. The game can be extended so that a child is on two shapes at once, or you may call out a shape for  the child to sit on. Continue until all the shapes are covered and begin again. Emphasize the correct use of vocabulary.

continued

The Guessing Box

Put an eraser in a shoe box and seal the box with masking tape. Pass the box among the children and ask them to guess what is in the box. They may do anything to the box that doesn't destroy it or open it. As the children are passing the box around, talk about guesses. Discuss which ones are impossible because the item guessed is either too heavy or too large to fit into the box. Discuss the possible correct guesses that correspond to the size, weight and sound of the item in the box. Open the box to see if a correct guess was given. Play the game again with a variety of hidden objects. Objects that make noise when the box is shaken add another type of clue.

How Big Is the Moon

To show the relative size of the Earth to the moon, blow up balloons to these relative sizes. A playground ball or basketball would represent the Earth, and a tennis ball or an orange would represent the moon. To show how far the moon is from the Earth, measure the circumference of your Earth model with strings. The distance between the moon and the Earth is about ten times this distance. Have the children take turns holding the Earth and moon the correct distance apart. Label the balloons and suspend them the correct distance apart in the room.

Whose Feet Are These

For this activity you will need a dog's paw print on a piece of paper. Ask the children if they know whose foot belongs to the footprint. The children may guess quickly that it is a dog's footprint. Ask them how they knew. Point out that footpads, toenails and the number of toes help identify a certain animal. Have footprints of a cat, chicken, duck, mouse and turtle available. (Footprints can be found in encyclopedias and Boy Scout products.) Discuss how each of these footprints is different. The different variety of footprints will also lead to a discussion of the many ways animals use their feet.

FINGER

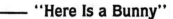

─────────────────────────── **"Here Is a Bunny"** ───────────────────────────

"Here is a bunny (make a fist)
With ears so funny (wiggle two fingers)
And here is a hole in the ground (make hole with other hand)
When a noise he hears
He picks up his ears (extend fingers fully)
And jumps in the hole in the ground.

Here comes a bunny (have children hop)
Hip - hop - hop
See how his long ears (put arms overhead and wave back and forth)
Flip - flop - flop
See how his nose goes (make fist, place over nose and squeeze)
Twink - twink - twink
See how his eyes go
Wink - wink - wink." (blink eyes)

─────────────────────────── **Dyeing Eggs** ───────────────────────────

For best results, use a commercial dye kit and follow the instructions on the packet. Here are different ways of dyeing hard-boiled eggs to make them your very own.

Crayon Resist: Draw a design or write your name with a white crayon. Dip the egg in the dye and watch your design appear.

Checked, Striped, Plaid: String, strips of tape and rubber bands placed securely around the eggs and then dipped into dye make interesting designs.

Batik: Drip some melted wax from a birthday candle on the shell of the egg. Dip the egg into the dye. Remove and scrape off the wax.

Egg Carton Caterpillar

Collect egg cartons made of fiber. Remove the tops from the carton and discard. With scissors, cut the bottom sections of the carton in half lengthwise leaving two long strips, each having six egg "cups." Turn the strips over so the "cups" are upside down. Trim the edges of the strip. Paint with tempera paint. Add pipe cleaner antennas and you will have a caterpillar.

Eggshell Pictures

Save the eggshells from dyed Easter eggs and crush into small pieces. Keep the colors in separate containers. Draw a picture or a design on a piece of paper. Put glue on a small area and press the shells into the glue. Proceed with the next area until the design or picture is completed.

Pretzel Wall Hanging

Cut a piece of yellow or blue burlap 13 x 4 inches. Cut a plastic straw into a 4-inch length, fold the top of the burlap around it and glue in place. Paste straight pretzels, twisted pretzels and fancy-shaped cereals into an interesting design on the burlap. Run a length of yarn through the straw and knot to make a hanger.

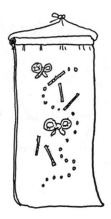

continued

Easter Egg Cards

Fold a piece of white construction paper in half. Draw an egg, with the top of the egg on the fold. Cut the egg out and decorate it. Children can color the outside of the egg with crayons, felt tip pens or paint. Punch dots out of colored paper, or eggshells can be glued to the outside of the card. Write "Happy Easter" on a rectangle of colored paper and have the children sign the card.

Paper Plate Rabbit

Use two 9-inch white paper plates. One plate will be the rabbit's head. Cut the other plate into an hourglass shape. The hourglass shape will become the rabbit's bow tie. The two outside edges of the plate will become the rabbit's ears. Cut eyes, nose and whiskers out of construction paper or have the children draw them on with felt tip pens. Glue the ears and bow tie to the rabbit's face. The children can also glue on cotton balls to make him soft and furry. Tie a piece of yarn to the top of the rabbit's head so that it can be hung.

Easter Bunny

Glue a 2-inch Styrofoam egg to a pair of feet cut out of pink construction paper. Paste two paper punch holes (from blue construction paper) on the egg to represent the bunny's eyes. Stick two chenille pipe cleaners (4 inches long) on top for his ears. Cut two 3-inch pieces of pink curling ribbon. Tie the ribbon in the middle, fringe the ends and glue on the egg to make the bunny's whiskers.

Egg People

When cracking eggs, open at one end. Place emptied eggshell, open end up, on a small collar of construction paper. Carefully draw eyes, nose and mouth with a felt tip pen. Place a wet cotton ball inside the egg and sprinkle with grass seed. Place the eggs on windowsills. Keep the cotton ball moist. Watch your egg people grow hair.

continued

------------------------------ **Soft Pretzels** ------------------------------

In a large bowl soften:
1 package yeast in 1¼ cups lukewarm water
Add ¾ teaspoon salt and 1½ teaspoons sugar to yeast mixture. Add 4 cups flour to mixture and knead into a soft dough. Do not let the dough rise. Immediately cut into small pieces and roll into slender ropes. (Do not make ropes too thick because they will swell in baking.) Twist ropes into pretzel shapes and lay them in a foil-covered cookie sheet dusted with flour. Brush with beaten egg and sprinkle coarse salt over them. Bake at 400° until golden brown. Makes 3-6 dozen pretzels.

Matzo

Mix and knead 3½ cups flour and 1 cup water. Roll out the dough on a floured surface and transfer to a greased cookie sheet. Prick all over with a fork and score into squares with a knife. Bake at 475° for 10 to 15 minutes until lightly browned.

Charoses

1 cup chopped apples
¼ cup chopped nuts
1 teaspoon cinnamon
2 tablespoons grape juice

Mix all ingredients together and use as a tasty spread for matzo.

Macaroons
(made with matzo meal)

4 egg whites
¾ cup sugar
1½ teaspoons matzo meal
1 cup coconut
1½ teaspoons lemon juice
1¼ teaspoons potato starch

TO LEARN

Beat egg whites and sugar and add remaining ingredients. Spoon onto a greased cookie sheet and bake until brown, about 20 minutes at 325°.

Brown, Margaret Wise. **The Golden Egg Book.** New York: Simon & Schuster, 1947.
> Colorful pictures illustrate a lonely little bunny who finds an egg which eventually hatches out a lonely little duck.

Carrick, Carol. **A Rabbit for Easter.** New York: Greenwillow Books, 1979.
> Paul takes care of his kindergarten's pet rabbit Sam over Easter vacation, and almost loses him because he forgets to lock the cage.

Carroll, Ruth. **Where's the Bunny?** Ithaca, NY: Walck & Rikhoff, 1950.
> Bunny and Puppy wake up and enjoy playing together until bedtime, when Puppy tries to find Bunny.

Duvoisim, Roger. **Easter Treat.** New York: Knopf, 1954.
> Santa Claus goes on his Easter vacation dressed in street clothes; but is so well disguised, the children in the city do not believe him when he tells them who he is.

Fisher, Aileen. **Easter.** New York: Thomas Y. Crowell, 1968.
> The story of Easter is traced back to the worldwide celebration of springtime, ending with the story of Jesus of Nazareth.

Politi, Leo. **Juanita.** New York: Scribner, 1948.
> Juanita gets a dove for her birthday and anxiously awaits Easter, when "The Blessing of the Animals" takes place.

Simon, Norma. **Passover.** New York: Thomas Y. Crowell, 1965.
> This book gives an account of the Jews' suffering under the Pharaohs and their flight from Egypt, followed by ways in which the holiday is celebrated today.

Weil, Lisl. **The Candy Egg Bunny.** New York: Holiday House, 1975.
> Skeptical Walter meets the Candy Egg Bunny, who tells him why the Bunny gives candy eggs to children at Eastertime.

Decorate the Easter eggs by coloring the circles blue, the diamonds red and the squares yellow.

Cut and paste the place setting on the table for a festive Seder feast.

Planning and Carrying Out Daily Activities

If an activity is generated and partially completed by the teacher, the end result should be something children can use for pleasure and happiness on their own. The teacher may want to use these activities for group instruction. (Example: masks made from paper plates can be used in songs, and later for the children to use in their own imaginative play.)

The self-satisfaction that children feel by doing something on their own should be the goal of any activity. Plan activities that are possible for the toddler to accomplish. Remember, many of the best things that are done with toddlers don't go home in hand. They go home in head and heart, which is so much more important.

When singing with toddlers, remember the key is repetition. Sing favorite songs again and again, day after day. Quiet music played during rest time should include well-known, favorite songs. When a song is accompanied by motions, the toddlers will first learn the motions and later to sing the song. It is not uncommon for the teacher to be the only one singing the first couple of times. Remember, toddlers don't learn all the words at once; they begin by singing only key words.

Here are hints to help you handle some typical problems with toddlers.

Situation: Two toddlers want the same toy.
Solutions: "What **else** can **you** use?"
"What **can we find** for her/him?"
"Here's **another** car for **you** to use."
"**She needs** the choo-choo now."
"**Let's set** the time for two minutes,
then it will be your turn."

Situation: One toddler begins hurting another.
Solutions: "Billy **does not** like to be hit. **It hurts!**"
"We **only** bite **food**. Biting people **hurts!**"

Situation: Toddler refuses to cooperate.
Solutions: "You **need to sit** at the table."
"He **has to have** that chair."
"**You forgot** to throw away your napkin."
"It's **time to** wash hands now."
"I will **help you** put it away."
"I will **watch you** put it away."

Always tell a toddler what behavior you expect. Never ask if he or she wants to do it. Asking can invite negativism. Also, show a toddler how to play by participating with him or her. Be alert and anticipate problems, and step in to prevent them from occurring. (Example: "Hold your glass with **two** hands!") When talking to toddlers, specific, simple, concrete words are best.

Be sure to remember:

1. Large muscle control preceeds fine motor coordination, so select toys and activities which emphasize larger movements rather than fine finger control.
2. Growth comes in spurts and toddlers will focus on one kind of task more than others, so never expect all children to participate in an activity.
3. Toddlers rarely play together, but usually play beside someone else or alone, even though they tend to gather in one spot.
4. Toddlers do not understand someone else's point of view; therefore, toddlers can be helped to begin to understand by saying such things as, "It hurts her when you pinch," or "Jason needs the horsie now."
5. Toddlers love to imitate. Teachers should attempt to be models of acceptable behavior. Also, imitation helps the child remember and form mental pictures of something or someone who is not present. That is why a housekeeping area for play helps the toddler feel at home and comfortable.
6. Toddlers are often extreme in their actions due to their neurological immaturity, not due to willfullness. A toddler tends to grasp too strongly and release with overextension (throwing movement). Sometimes, they simply cannot let go. A toddler might withhold elimination too long and have an "explosive" accident on the way to the bathroom. Mood swings are common. A toddler may turn quickly from laughing to whining; active play to passive thumb sucking. Be patient and understanding.
7. Toddlers crave repetition and constancy in activities and daily patterns, so a daily schedule of routines is very important to a preschooler's feelings of security and self. Toddlers tolerate very little fluctuation of routine.

Sample Lesson Plan

Instructions for the activities listed in the following one day's lesson plan are found in the unit "Family and Friends." The size of groups and number of groups are flexible. Write lesson plans to suit your own situation. The lesson plan given is based on two groups of children.

Time	2-3½ Year Olds	3½-5 Year Olds
Opening of school	Free play in the room. Permanent centers will provide sufficient activities.	
8:30-8:45	Putting away and cleaning up of the centers.	
8:45-9:00	Everyone sitting in one area. Talk about the calendar, weather, current events, birthdays, helper board and limited "show and share" activities.	
9:00-9:20	Structured Activities—Divide into groups according to age and abilities of children.	
	bubble activity using commercial bubble product	sorting activity with uniform container
9:20-9:40	sorting activity using Tupperware container	bubble activity making soap solution from shampoo
9:40-9:50	Toilet break and washing of hands for snacks and cooking activity.	
9:50-10:00	Graham crackers and milk because of the cooking activity scheduled.	
10:00-10:20	Cooking Activity—Make "finger jello" for afternoon snack.	
10:20-11:00	Outdoor play.	
11:00-11:30	Group Experience—Spend time on carpeted area (can involve stories, music, puppets, creative dramatics, etc.) Share family pictures of the class and put them on the bulletin board. Learn two finger plays. (Finger plays written on 3 x 5 inch cards can be handled easily by the teacher on the rug and put into an apron pocket when not needed.)	
11:30-12:00	Lunch	
12:00-2:00	Nap time and outdoor time.	
2:00-2:15	Juice and snack time. Eat "finger jello" made in the morning activity.	
2:15-3:00	Art Activity and Cleanup—Finger-paint on tabletop. Make print to take home.	
3:00-Closing time	Indoor/outdoor play time.	

Permanent Classroom Centers

Each classroom should have a center for:
- Housekeeping (kitchen, dress-up clothes, mirrors, dolls, dishes)
- Store (counter, empty cans, cash register)
- Easel Painting (easels, tempera paints, large brushes, smocks, newsprint paper)
- Building Center (blocks, Tinkertoys, Legos)
- Reading Center (books, puzzles, quiet games)
- Science Shelf (seed experiments, seashells, interesting critters and visiting pets)
- Toy Center (trucks, farm sets, miscellaneous goodies)
- Bulletin Board(s) (calendar, helpers, weather, notices, current unit, families)

Cooking To Learn

Cooking is an excellent learning activity in itself. It develops concepts of measuring, understanding of scientific principles and motor coordination. If you plan to cook, allow enough time for the preparation and baking or cooking of the item. If the item cannot be eaten after the preparation, it can be eaten for the afternoon snack or for tomorrow's morning snack.

Remember, the younger the child, the longer the preparation time. But children, if given the opportunity to use the peeler, grater, egg beater, spoon or fork, will learn to handle these items safely to produce something they can enjoy. After all, this is the purpose of the cooking activity. Safety is primary, but can be taught along with the use of tools.

Sample Language Activities

Many activities during the course of the day reinforce skills that are specifically taught in the daily lessons.

- Vigorous free play indoors and outdoors, plus climbing, jumping, riding wheel toys and follow-the-leader games, provide opportunities for increased development of large motor skills.
- Free play activities with blocks, manipulative toys, puzzles, Tinkertoys, serving food, setting the table, watering the plants and dressing and undressing, help reinforce small muscle control.
- Encouraging children to tell stories and to talk about anything of interest, especially during "show and share" time, help increase development of language skills and vocabulary.

235

Special activities

Birthdays are special occasions that deserve special recognition. The child's birthday or the day nearest to it can be made special by making a "birthday hat" for the child to wear during the school day and to take home later. The hat can be made from a 12 x 18 inch sheet of construction paper. Fold a 3-inch length of the paper back. This forms the brim of the hat. On the brim, write "Happy Birthday _____." Fold the length back into a cone and staple. Staple flowers to the cone or cut ¼-inch strips of construction paper and curl them around a pencil. These can be tucked into the brim and serve as feathers. Appropriate cut-out construction paper pictures can be stapled to the middle of the brim. They could be a facial profile of a girl or boy or a cake with the correct number of candles on it. Use a black felt tip pen to write the age of the child in the middle of the picture. Keep a couple of boxes of frozen cupcakes or donuts in the freezer for a quick "birthday cake" for treat time.

Bringing something home from school to share with the family is another special activity that children enjoy. A satchel or "suitcase" containing a book or puzzle of the child's choice, along with two or three other activities (pasting, matching, sorting) favorite records and articles of interest for the parents, are examples of items that can be included in the "suitcase." Each child has a chance to have a turn to share the suitcase with his or her family for several days.

Sharing the school experience with parents is a rewarding event for both the child and parents. A shortened version of a regular day held on a Saturday morning, usually for two hours, gives parents a chance to see what goes on at school and students a chance to better bridge the gap between home and school.

Sample Counting Activities

Counting objects of interest such as dolls, blocks, cookies, cups and napkins, especially during snack time, and having the children manipulate these items, helps the understanding of number concepts. Counting is reinforced in this way and also extended through the use of calendars, charts, scales and rulers in the classroom.

Sample Pupil Information Form

Family History

Child's Name_____ Nickname_____

Address _____

Home Telephone_____ Birthdate_____

Mother's Name _____

Mother's present occupation (if employed) _____

Mother's former occupation _____

Mother's business address_____ Telephone_____

Father's name _____

Father's occupation _____

Father's business address_____ Telephone_____

Are parents divorced? _____

Name, age and sex of other children in the family _____

_____

_____

Religious Affiliation (Both Parents)_____

(If any of the children are adopted, please indicate which ones.)

_____

Sleeping

What time does he usually go to bed at night?_____ Get up in the morning?_____

Does he take a daytime nap or rest?_____ If so, for how long?_____

Speech

Does he speak plainly so that others besides those at home can understand him?_____

Are any foreign languages spoken in the home?_____

Toilet

When your child has to use the toilet, what term does he use? _____

PUPIL INFORMATION FORM
continued

Personality

Does he have any special fears?_____ If so, please list and explain. _____

_____

_____

Are you aware of any special problems, such as aggression, anger, anxiety, hostility, etc.? _____

_____

Discipline

By what means do you "discipline" your child? By spanking?_____ By scolding?_____

By putting to bed?_____ Other ways?_____

Miscellaneous

Is there any information which we should have concerning your child which would help us to understand him better? _____

_____

_____

_____

What are you hoping to have your child gain from this experience? _____

_____

_____

_____

What previous group experiences has your child had?_____

_____

_____

Are there others living in your household? If so, please list. _____

_____

_____

Father_____

Mother_____

Sample Health Information Form

Emergency Health Record (to be filled out by parent)

Name_____ Age_____ Sex (M)_____ (F)_____

Address_____ Zip_____

Birthplace_____ Birthdate_____

Parent or Guardian_____ Home Phone_____

Father's Business Phone_____ Mother's Business Phone_____

In case of emergency: If Parents or Guardian are not immediately available contact:

Friend or Relative_____ Phone_____

Physician_____ Phone_____

Hospital_____ Phone_____

In case of emergency, the school may call the family physician to examine my son or daughter.

(Without such permission, the school assumes no responsibility for emergency medical attention.)

Yes_____ No_____

Signature of parent or guardian_____

Date_____

Medical Record

Name of child's doctor _____

Address _____

Serious accidents _____

Serious illnesses _____

_____

Operations _____

Hospitalization _____

Handicaps (eyes, ears, feet, etc.) _____

_____

Allergies _____

_____

Communicable Diseases: Please check the diseases which your child has had and give date.

_____Chicken Pox   Date:_____   _____German Measles   Date:_____

_____Infectious Hepatitis Date:_____   _____Red Measles   Date:_____

_____Mumps   Date:_____   _____Rheumatic Fever   Date:_____

_____Whooping Cough   Date:_____